ENDORSEMENTS

As Executive Director of the Napoleon Hill Foundation, I always teach others that success begins in the mind. Our thoughts truly direct our lives, but we don't always realize how important our mental health is to success. In Better Hands is a valuable tool that will show you how to succeed with life no matter what your past looks like.

—**DON GREEN,** the Executive Director of the Napoleon Hill Foundation

"I've always felt that true strength is found in vulnerability; In Better Hands is the exemplification of that statement. The author creates an atmosphere of raw emotion that will have you crying at times and at others, smiling at the nostalgia brought on by her words. In Better Hands will inspire you to reach out to the world in an authentic and beautiful way."

—**STEPHANIE STROUTH,** LPC, Owner of Anchoring Hope Counseling

in better hands

AN APPALACHIAN MEMOIR
OF HEALING AND GRACE

in better
hands

AN APPALACHIAN MEMOIR
OF HEALING AND GRACE

FORWARD PUBLISHING

Contact information for Forward Publishing – forwardpublisher@gmail.com

ISBN: 979-8-9887925-0-5 (paperback)
ISBN: 979-8-9887925-1-2 (ebook)

Library of Congress Control Number: 2023913997

Printed in Wise, Virginia

Ordering Information:
Special discounts are available on quantity purchases by corporations, associations, and others. For details, contact https://www.brandicoxauthor.com

Cover photo by Jessica Leigh Hood

Interior artwork by Ashlyn Mullins

Publisher's Cataloging-in-Publication Data

Names: Cox, Brandi, 1979- .
Title: In better hands : an Appalachian memoir of healing and grace / Brandi Cox.
Description: Wise, VA : Forward Publishing, 2024. | Summary: A true story of sorrow, growth, and understanding, this memoir shares an inspiring journey to find peace after abandonment, adoption, and grief.
Identifiers: LCCN 2023913997 | ISBN 9798988792505 (pbk.) | ISBN 9798988792512 (ebook)
Subjects: LCSH: Cox, Brandi, 1979- . | Adoptees – Biography. | Addicts – Biography. | Healing. | Psychic trauma. | Appalachian Region – Biography. | BISAC: BIOGRAPHY & AUTOBIOGRAPHY / Personal Memoirs. | BIOGRAPHY & AUTOBIOGRAPHY / Women. | BIOGRAPHY & AUTOBIOGRAPHY / Cultural, Ethnic & Regional / General.
Classification: LCC HV874.82.C69 2024 | DDC 920.72 C--dc23
LC record available at https://lccn.loc.gov/2023913997

Author's Notes

Healing is the most beautiful thing you can do for yourself and your family! Realizing that you are worthy of a brighter future without concern for your past is liberating; you are permitting yourself to explore your goals to take on life with a positive and focused mindset.

I wrote this book to bring awareness to mental illness, addictions, and suicide. Without understanding, nothing will change, and without change, there is not much hope for those who struggle. Mental illness is a disease, much like cancer or heart disease. Instead of being recognized as such, it is treated as an outlier. It is not just the person with the mental illness and/or addiction that struggles; it is also the entire family.

Not only do I hope to promote awareness for those suffering, but I also hope to encourage anyone who is dealing with depression and low self-worth. You are worthy of chasing your dreams. Neither your past nor your family dictates your future. Do not allow fear to hold you back any longer.

In Better Hands recounts my memories and a timeline constructed through my conversations with family members. Four of the five main characters in the story are deceased, so some information cannot be verified. I consulted with my brother and two aunts regarding some memories and timelines and incorporated them into the manuscript. The memories I have shared of John are only those relatable to my story. I did not include other friends or family members who were not directly connected to my stories or did not want to be included. All names have been changed to protect their privacy. In certain instances, revealing characteristics have also been removed. I altered some locations to protect those involved from being identified.

Please be advised that this story has triggers such as adoption, alcohol addiction, suicide, and death.

Table of Contents

Cast of Characters

John: my birth father
Karen: my birth mom
Joyce: paternal grandmother—my adopted mother
Richard: paternal grandfather—my adopted father
William: paternal uncle—my brother by adoption
Nicole: paternal cousin—my niece by adoption
Aunt Donna: my aunt
David: my brother by my birth mom
Heather: my lifelong best friend
Stephanie: a friend in middle and high school

Preface

Throughout the years, I have questioned if I was a product of my raising, biology, or a mixture of both. So many people overlooked what I experienced as a child—the sounds of screams, the tears, and the silence still haunt me. Those experiences were at the root of my formation. So much of my inner value was based on what occurred in my early childhood.

A glimpse into my life showed two loving parents who thought I hung the moon, a nice home with all the comforts we could need, and an extended family that was supportive and loving.

Forgotten was the other set of parents who stayed in the background— the parents who chose not to raise me, the ones who walked away and left me with my paternal grandparents while my parents carried on with their lives. Between both of my birth parents, I have six half brothers and sisters who were not given up for adoption. Instead, they were raised by one or both parents. Leaving me to ask, "Why me?" That singular question, "Why wasn't I good enough?" perpetrated every portion of my life. I felt discarded and less than, as if I had done something wrong. I assumed I wasn't good enough since I was the only child given away. Therefore, I believed it to be so and required affirmations from others. I needed their approval, maybe not because I was afraid of being wrong but afraid they would leave if I made the wrong decision.

I was the epitome of fake it till you make it. Worried about being judged, I often mirrored others' reactions or reverberated their statements. In a sense, I was a human chameleon before I knew what that was. I altered and adjusted to blend in with whatever crowd I was hanging out with. I had done that for so long that I had no idea who I was or how I felt about anything.

My negative self-talk did far more damage to me than anything that anyone else said or did. Unlike someone else's fleeting comments, your internal conversation never turns off. So, if you are on the bashing-yourself train, you can guarantee it will have long-lasting effects. Overcoming who you believe you are is more challenging than showing others how wrong they are about you. It took me years to realize that I was my own worst enemy.

Finding the strength to believe in yourself is not for the weak—it's a powerful tool that will serve you throughout every avenue of your life. Allow yourself to let go of the past and fully accept that your future is only limited by you. Your family does not determine who you will be or what you will accomplish. The mistakes from the past do not eliminate the possibility of success in the future.

Accepting—no, embracing—that I was not held hostage by my past or my family's choices was liberating. For the first time, I permitted myself to strive for the goals I had always dreamed of. I knew I wanted to help others and make a difference in this world; to do that, I first had to fix myself. I am proof that childhood trauma can be overcome and that generational curses can be broken. Read along with me as I share a story of sorrow, growth, and understanding.

CHAPTER 1
Transcending the Past

He was also the man who put what was best for me before himself.

Incessant itching, sore throat, fatigue, and grotesque blisters were how I welcomed summer vacation. Instead of playing outside and riding my bike, I was constrained to the couch, and commandeering the TV was my only option for entertainment. Typically, the TV was always my jurisdiction except for Mom's 3 p.m. soap opera and Dad's nightly news. They both took pity on me during the most unfair week of my life, as I deemed it—the week I had chicken pox.

In the heat of the summer of 1986 my long brown hair was matted with sweat and ointment that were covering my body. Although I wore only one of Dad's thin white undershirts and a pair of panties, the sweat was still dripping from my face. The shirt stuck to the blisters, which caused continual moans whenever I moved. The combination of the ointment and sweat left a sticky mess that only encouraged further scratching. My face was red and blistered, with two blisters stacked upon each other on the bridge of my nose between my eyes, preventing me from wearing my glasses. My face was unrecognizable! All I could see were scabs from scratching or blisters.

With only a single window air conditioner to cool our entire 2,000+ square-foot home, the temperature difference between the rooms was nauseating while I was sick. I postponed bathroom trips to the back of the house until I felt as if my bladder could explode. Jumping up from the couch and scurrying through the dining room, I paid no mind to my surroundings. I didn't glance at either of the mirrors or my reflection in the china cabinet glass. I was on a mission with my head down to prevent anything from stopping me.

After using the bathroom, I wanted to see how my face was healing. I was seven years old, and my curiosity got the best of me. I walked over to the mirror and gasped! The next thing I remember was Mom helping me onto the bed. I fainted either from weakness or at the sight of myself. Either way, I have two scars between my eyebrows to commemorate that awful sickness.

Still groggy from fainting, I could see John pacing the floor between the living room and kitchen, peeking in to see how I looked. His face was as white as a ghost, and his eyes were huge, as he paused in the doorway for Mom to tell him I was okay. He didn't enter the bedroom; instead, he kept his distance out of shock and fear.

While I was resting on a stack of feather pillows with a cold washcloth laid across my forehead, Mom rushed off to the kitchen to fetch a fever reducer and a lemon wedge. I don't know the science behind the lemon wedge, but for some reason, it always relieved my nausea. I dozed off to sleep due to the combination of the steady rain, circulating fan, medicine, and cold washcloth.

After a short nap, I felt better, as good as I could with chicken pox. Like most kids, I was resilient while sick. Once the temperature was under control, I wanted to do something. John knew I couldn't venture far from the house, so while I was resting, he went to the garage and got two fishing poles ready for us to use.

Lying in bed, I heard the back door open and John holler, "Get your shoes on, Sissy. We're going fishing on the top road."

I thought he was crazy. There was no body of water near our house. How could we fish? Also, I didn't like fish, so I didn't want to touch them.

My lack of response didn't deter him from our fishing adventure. Instead, I think it made him and Mom act overly excited about it. They were both standing by my bed with silly smiles and raised eyebrows, look-ing crazy. They both used the silly adult, high-pitched voice to convince me it would be fun. I laughed at their excitement and reveled in the effort they were both putting forth to help me feel better. Seeing my shoes in Mom's hands, I resigned myself to the fishing adventure. Sitting up in the bed with eyebrows ruffled, I smiled at them both.

John said laughingly, "Don't worry. You will not have to touch or eat a single fish."

Okay, I didn't have to touch the fish—that's good. I didn't have to eat the fish—that's better. John wanted to spend time with me—that's great. I threw my feet out of the bed and onto the floor, only pausing to put my flip-flops on that Mom was holding. There was no mention of me changing my shirt, putting on shorts, or brushing my hair. They let me go out looking like a hot mess, and I didn't care either. We only had a few neighbors, and they wouldn't have judged me for looking like I did while I was sick.

I bounced up the driveway behind him, excited to be doing anything that wasn't lying in bed or on the couch. Once on the top road, we walked behind our neighbor's home, where a giant mud puddle had formed from the rain earlier that day. The sky was overcast and dreary, which worked out well for me. The sun would have been too painful on the sores.

He handed me the fishing pole and challenged me to a competition to catch the biggest fish. John patiently showed me how to cast and reel the fishing line back in. I am left-handed, so mimicking him was more complicated than I thought. My hands and fingers kept going in the wrong place. With every cast, I would say, "This one is it. I will catch the biggest fish ever." Of course, there were no fish in the mud puddle that had just formed earlier that day. But that didn't matter. I just enjoyed being with him. During those few hours, we laughed and talked. I felt like the most important person in the world to him.

So, who is John? He is my birth father, my Big Daddy. The man who couldn't stand to see me sick, the man who loved with his entire heart and made me feel like the most important person in the world. As a child, I watched him with wonder, admiring how his laugh filled a room and how his eyes sparkled as he chuckled.

He was also the man who put what was best for me before himself. You see, in the winter of 1979, his alcoholism led to the discussion of my adoption—love decided that my paternal grandparents would raise me. When I was three weeks old, my grandparents, Joyce and Richard, became my parents. My birth father, John, became my brother, and my birth mother, Karen, became an acquaintance.

The realignment of our family hierarchy ricocheted into my extended family. My paternal uncle, William, became my older brother. William was the eldest of the siblings and was viewed as a good child—the one who did well in school, played football, and stayed out of trouble.

My birth father, John, was multifaceted and challenging to understand. While sober, he was loving and funny—someone I wanted to be around. I liked the man who volunteered to drive me to school in the morning instead of making me walk, allowing me to get those extra few minutes of sleep. I wanted the father figure who made the joking comment that I wasn't allowed to date until I was in my 30s. That was the John we all wanted—who teased us with visits but didn't stay.

He was the handsome rebel who often lost his temper if alcohol was involved. With alcohol coursing through his veins and his inhibitions quashed, he gave little thought to how his actions would affect him or his family. His repetitive and outlandish decisions typically ended with him alienating more people or getting in trouble—often both.

John's bad choices started in primary school, around the age that children were learning to read. Picking up a book and sounding out words didn't come as easily to him as it did to others. Some words were jumbled-up messes in his eyes. Instead of confiding in a teacher or his mom, he masked the issue by acting out. At first his outbursts weren't volatile; they were funny and borderline disrespectful, like speaking out of turn in class, saying outlandish comments, or cracking jokes instead of answering his teacher's questions. His lack of interest in school was deemed misbehavior instead of a disability.

At some point, his teachers saw through John's behavior and, to some level, understood his rebellion. There was not a lot of guidance or programs to help children with dyslexia in the 1960s, and the teachers were doing their best. They did offer to help him with the resources available, but he was reluctant.

The class clown act did serve him well for a while—the kids thought he was funny and enjoyed having him around. The teachers avoided calling on him in class to keep the peace. Once John was a few years older, the teachers no longer cared about keeping the peace, and instead, they tried to force him to learn to read. That push was enough to cause John to change his tactics. Instead of being the class clown, he became the class bully. I suspect he became a bully to make sure the kids were afraid to laugh at him when he struggled in class or with his homework. Either way, his attitude was no longer excusable in the school system.

Assuming his actions would not progress further than the class bully, everyone focused on taming his attitude. As a 10-year-old boy with low self-esteem and high anxiety, John was drowning mentally. His calls for help were made through outbursts and inappropriate behavior. He was searching for a reprieve from the pain when an adult offered him alcohol. A trusted family friend and neighbor whom he looked up to started giving him alcohol without John's mom or dad knowing. He trusted this individual and had no reason to believe it would lead to years of heartache for him. As a child already struggling and looking for a way out, it was a perfect escape—until it wasn't.

The progression of burying his feelings went from class clown to bullying to alcoholism. As each phase no longer provided a reprieve from the real world, he looked for something new.

The cause for John's error in judgments was dyslexia, and drinking evolved from the need to cover up his shortcomings to a need that couldn't be met without a bottle.

He surrounded himself with people who encouraged his poor choices and laughed at his erratic behavior while drinking. He ran with the wrong group, but I do not blame them for his choices. He was responsible for every decision he made. If that group of friends had not been there or accepted him, he would have found someone else.

As an adult, I understand how his dyslexia was a bridge to alcohol. He was looking for something to drown his pain and embarrassment. Alcohol reduced his inhibitions and allowed him not to feel so insecure. While drinking, he held the attitude that he was 10 feet tall and bulletproof. His temper was fiery, and his tolerance for interaction was exceptionally low.

The drinking continued for several years before my parents had real verification of a problem. At 13, John was arrested for disorderly conduct at the pool hall in our hometown of Neon, Kentucky. I assume this was the first time our family saw John's anger rear its ugly head while paired with alcohol. His antagonistic attitude and lack of cooperation caused the officers to beat him. John was not the type to back down from a fight, even a fight he couldn't win. When Dad picked him up from jail the following day, John's body and face showed signs of the previous night's altercation. This scare with the state police did not change his life's trajectory. It seemed to have little effect on him to have been arrested at age 13.

After his arrest, John began to push his boundaries further. He was more unruly and took larger risks. One of those risks ended with him being arrested in West Virginia when he and his cousin Billy Joe stole William's motorcycle from a locked shed in their backyard. That joy ride landed them in a town in West Virginia, going the wrong way on a one-way street. After being arrested, John's dad was called to come and pick them up. At the time, John didn't show remorse or regret for stealing the motorcycle—he seemed empowered and emboldened. He knew that his mom and dad would always come to his rescue.

CHAPTER 2

The Pain of Love

Mom and Dad both carried a different heavy burden that the other struggled to understand when it came to keeping John out of trouble.

John wasn't raised in a family that drank alcohol. Joyce and Richard's home was always alcohol-free except for the occasional cousin who brought some in, and even then our parents didn't drink. They were soft spoken and not combative or argumentative. So, for John to be so different was hard for them to understand.

Our dad, Richard, was the enforcer, the encourager, and the one you could depend on. No matter what, he was there for all of us and his extended family. He didn't shy away from his responsibilities; instead, he approached everything with the same perspective and attitude. He held himself to a very high standard that few could ever measure up to. He believed that a man should be an honest provider and worker. Dad lived those beliefs every day. He worked without complaint on days that he was sick and days that he was exhausted.

Being a coal miner was not for the faint of heart. Dad would rise long before the sun came up, dress in old dirt-stained clothes, pack a cold lunch, and drive an hour or more to work each morning. He would park his vehicle in a dirt lot, gather his belongings, place his hard hat upon his head, and enter the dark hole where he would spend the rest of his day.

Some of the mines Dad worked in were so shallow that he had to crawl or scoot through certain areas. Other mines were tall enough for men to hunch over, but they weren't able to stand up for hours on end. All the same, he worked eight- to 12-hour shifts running equipment, digging coal, and bracing walls to bring home an honest day's pay.

After spending a full day's work inside the mines, he would come home, sometimes grab a snack, and then go to his garden where he would weed, hoe, or harvest vegetables for the fall and winter. He was a hardworking man with little to no free time.

Even with all his work responsibilities that he valued highly, he still always made time for us, even when the times were not good. So, when he received the call to pick up John and Billy Joe in West Virginia, he dropped his other responsibilities and went. It wasn't a short, easy drive. Instead it was several hours each way on a curvy two-lane road between two mountains. He had to be mentally and physically exhausted, but he didn't complain; instead, he just went.

Joyce, our mom was the nurturer, supporter, and worrier of our family. She loved John so much, and with every instance of his poor decisions, she felt more helpless. Her daily tasks were never completed. Being a stay-at-home mom, she was responsible for us kids, the home, dinner, and bills, and somehow, she kept everything together. Even on the hard days, she pushed forward and met her duties. Dinner was always prepared and on the table every evening, while still making time to talk with us. She wanted to know about our days, both the good and bad.

Mom was a smaller woman who didn't like confrontation, so I wonder if she was afraid of what John would do if she confronted him. Or maybe he was her baby, and she was praying that her love could change him. Even when she had been pushed as far as she could go, confronting John only encouraged him to make another irrational decision. She was in a situation where there was no correct answer.

Mom and Dad both carried a different heavy burden that the other struggled to understand when it came to keeping John out of trouble. Mom felt overwhelmed because she was the one dealing with the day-to-day incidents. Dad felt guilty because he was unable to help due to his long hours at work. All three of them were on a merry-go-round that wouldn't slow down. The older John got, the harder it was for Mom to control him. He had a mind of his own and wasn't going to listen to her or anyone else. Every school morning, she would watch him walk through the front door of the high school, assuming he was staying in class for the day. Unfortunately, he would go through the front door, down the hallway past the lockers, and out the back door. From there he would go into town or to a buddy's house to spend the day.

John hated school and the strict routine and rules that accompanied it. For him, it was a form of prison that he no longer wanted any part of. Therefore, he didn't graduate. He dropped out of school without the blessing of his parents. Of course, they wanted him to stay in school and graduate, but they also knew they could not force him to finish.

Unlike Mom and Dad, John had the opportunity to finish high school, but instead he squandered it. Dad chose to drop out of school before he was old enough to read so that he could help his family financially. As a young child, he accepted any job, without concern for his own health or pride. To provide heat for his parents and siblings, he ran alongside the road to pick up coal that had fallen off the coal trucks. He started working outside the mines, shoveling coal well before he was old enough to go inside the deep, dark hole dug into a mountainside.

Because of his work ethic, he continued to be promoted in the mines without a formal education or the ability to read. Others, including my mom, helped him study for his electrician test, which he passed because the proctor read the questions out loud to him. Others realized that his intelligence and ability were far greater than his limitations. He went into work every day and gladly accepted overtime without ever considering what the strenuous labor was doing to his young body.

Mom was also forced to drop out of school prior to graduation. Her older sister was diagnosed with terminal cancer and required full-time care for herself and her four small children. So, Mom became a caregiver and nanny for her sister and children without hesitation. She formed a deep bond with her niece and nephews, a bond that grew stronger with each year. In some ways they viewed her as a second mom, while she viewed them as her kids. Donna, the only girl, was often spoiled by my parents. She was their little girl way before I was born.

Not having a formal education did not hold my parents back from building a good life for them and our family. Their main drive stemmed from the desire to give their children and grandchildren every opportunity they didn't have. Neither of our parents resented their choice of dropping out of school to help their families. They didn't blame others for their choices. Instead they just accepted it and treasured the lessons learned.

The only comment they ever made about an education was that if they had completed school, together they would have been unstoppable. That's so true because with the schooling they had, they were a force.

Most of us push forward through hard times and strive to be better because of dreams or goals that we have. Those goals keep us looking forward to their completion, so we don't have the time to worry about our mistakes. I cannot recall a single dream of John's that has been shared with me. You know—the dreams you fantasize about as a child, such as becoming a doctor, a nurse, or a police officer. I wonder if he could have seen a way to his future, a way that he could have been successful, would he have changed? Were his dreams too great for him to see small wins? Or was he void of dreams because of his addiction? These are all questions I wish I could answer. I wish I knew what was in his heart and mind.

I believe dreams and goals are what make us better people. When you have big, outlandish goals, you prioritize your time, you focus on what is important, and you immerse yourself in obtaining that goal. There is no time to focus on excuses or negativity. If only John saw himself as more capable, maybe everything would have been different.

For someone who had no interest in completing his education and could not stop his habitual drinking, John had a work ethic that was second to none when he was sober. The same Neon police officer who arrested John several times also worked with him in a coal mine somewhere in

Eastern Kentucky. His words to me gave me great pride in my birth father.

He said, "Brandi, he was one of the hardest-working men I had ever worked with. Even on the days that he had drunk too much the night before, he still showed up and did his job."

Since I was part of a family that was raised on the premise of hard work and responsibility, that gave me a sense of pride. Our dad worked nonstop every day and expected everyone else to put in the same effort. John was indeed Dad's son. Had he completed his education and been able to stop his bad habits, there's no telling what his life would have been like today.

CHAPTER 3

The Vicious Cycle

Fighting your own inner monologue is exhausting. Falling
back on a crutch that serves to remove the negative
thoughts is easy, it alleviates the pain temporarily.

Every family that faces addiction reacts differently. My parents went through the phases of denial, negative reinforcement, strict punishment, begging, pleading, and support. Of course, they rotated back and forth between each of these, praying for one of them to work. I assume these phases are common for family members who help their loved ones fight an addiction.

I pause and think of the emotions and pain that all three of them felt simultaneously, and my heart breaks. None of them wanted this life. None of them asked for it. It was a life by circumstance that all of them were chained to. Dyslexia and low self-esteem led to John's alcohol addiction. The low self-worth and anger, paired with alcohol, led to outbursts that were uncontrollable.

John's drinking became more serious and volatile with each passing year. His once-social drinking converted to anger and fights. His reckless decisions while drinking were a constant worry for his family. He was frequently drinking and driving without a thought for others' safety. He would appear on his parents' doorstep, reeking of alcohol and barely able to stand up. They never knew where he had been on those nights. They only knew that he was extremely inebriated and lucky that he had not hurt himself or someone else.

After a rough day, I think of how I instinctively want to have a drink, and I assume that is how it started for John. For him, the "I will just have one drink to calm my nerves," turned into 10 drinks. The "I'm only drinking occasionally," turned into daily. The "I'm only drinking socially," turned into drinking alone. I wonder if my ability to not overdrink or become addicted to alcohol is because of the memories I have of my birth father.

I think of how easy it could be to fall into a vicious cycle of addiction. Dealing with inner demons isn't easy. Fighting your own inner monologue is exhausting. Falling back on a crutch that serves to remove the negative thoughts is easy, it alleviates the pain temporarily. The difference is some coping mechanisms are healthy, and some are unhealthy. John was coping, unhealthily, but coping all the same.

After several run-ins with law enforcement because of alcohol, John was sent to a rehab facility in Cumberland, Kentucky. Mom and Dad saw this as an opportunity for John to get the help he needed. It was a chance for him to heal and recover without the negative distractions around him. Our parents dropped him off one afternoon with a bittersweet goodbye. It's never easy leaving your baby, even if they need to be left. Unfortunately, they received a phone call a few days later requesting that they pick up John. He had broken the rules by drinking. When they arrived, he was crying and upset, swearing that he would change.

John shoveled excuses to Mom and Dad, blaming everyone else at the center for his inability to say no to the alcohol that was snuck into the facility. "The aides did not like me, so they set me up." "The aide said it was okay for me to drink if I didn't tell anyone." "I needed the drink—everything was too hard in the center."

I assume the third reason was the truth—that he needed the alcohol, just as we need air." I say "needed" instead of "wanted" because for someone truly addicted to alcohol, it is a need—a painful physical urge that is hard to eradicate. If offered the one vice that takes away your pain, it's difficult to say no.

I still struggle with the decision of the facility to kick John out of rehab for breaking the rule of drinking. He was placed in this facility to help him break a habit that he couldn't break on his own. His willpower to overcome a physical and mental addiction to alcohol wasn't strong enough when surrounded by temptation. This facility was his chance to turn his life around, and someone took that away from him.

Someone snuck alcohol into the facility and shared it with him. I have no idea who the culprit was who did such a cruel act, but I hope they know all the lives that were affected by it. I don't blame John because he was there for help. If he could have kicked the habit with temptation in front of him, rehab wouldn't have been needed.

The disappointment that both parents felt on their way to pick up John was palpable. They had so hoped that his time away would help break the unbreakable cycle that he was struggling with. All they wanted was the son that they knew and loved to be whole again. Dad was exhausted by the constant worrying and fighting with John. Dad's job as a coal miner was already physically and emotionally demanding, so his capacity to handle much else was low. It was difficult for Dad to make two trips to Cumberland in such proximity, but he did it.

Mom was mentally exhausted and heartbroken because of John's continual drinking and disregard for the repercussions. She and Dad were already at odds on how to deal with John and his consistent drinking. Dad was more of the hard disciplinarian, and Mom was the one who would be more hurt than mad.

After returning home, John sank deeper into despair and depression. Certain that he had no chance of turning his life around, he started down a darker and more harmful road that there was no returning from.

In 1978 John's temper was growing uncontrollable when he was drinking, but he had never been physically abusive to Mom. No matter what was said between them, he never touched her or gave the impression that he would, until one morning in the kitchen when Mom was home alone. He was not accustomed to his requests being met with resistance from

Mom. For whatever reason, that morning was different. She took a stance with a resounding no, which caused John's anger to erupt. She was usually a pushover when it came to him, typically meeting every request either out of fear or love, and when she didn't, he was blinded by anger. Without hesitation, John grabbed Mom's arm and pulled her closer to him so hard that he dislocated her shoulder.

Mom said that John's eyes were huge, as if they would pop out of his head. His mouth gaped open, and his breathing increased to the point of panic. Instead of staying there to help her or make amends for what he had done, he jetted out the back door and into his car. To think that John's temper could ever escalate to being physically aggressive toward Mom was inconceivable.

After he sobered up, tears flowed like a child as he begged her to forgive him. He was devastated at the thought of hurting her. She was the person always there for him and essentially cleaned up the messes he created. She was the one who tried to smooth over his erratic behavior with family and friends when he treated them poorly. Indeed, she was his best and strongest ally. Mom told me later that she blamed it on the alcohol, that if he had been sober, he wouldn't have hurt her. I believe that is true. The alcohol changed him into a different person, someone who was angry and violent.

William recounted an argument between Dad and John that occurred shortly before I was born that still gives me chills. John was already buzzed and combative toward both of our parents, for reasons we are not sure of. John yelled at Dad, "You don't care about me or anything I do. You just want to pick fights with me."

Dad firmly responded, "John, I just want you to act right. Stop this nonsense."

Dad was not a pushover and would not back down from John. This argument escalated to John pulling out a 20-gauge side-by-side double-barrel shotgun and shooting the hat off Dad's head. Dad grabbed the gun from him and held it tightly before it could be used again as he yelled, "Damn it, son. This stops now." John tore out of the house in a fit of anger. Dad was shaking all over, with his face as red as blood. Mom said she thought he may explode because he was so angry.

I think about the adrenaline and anger that was swirling in the room. I can't imagine watching your own child shoot a gun at you in your own home—a son whom you have raised and cared for, a son who was never treated unfairly by you. Yet you receive the brunt of his anger. Dad never spoke of this incident to me; I assume to protect me and John's memory. Family should be a form of shelter and safety, not the attacker.

Mom never said if John apologized to Dad or if everything just went back to "normal" after John sobered up. John was so different when he wasn't drinking that I'm sure it had to bother him. He had to feel remorse and sadness for his irrational actions. Dad and John's relationship had been tumultuous for years—they both had different views on life and how one should conduct themself. So, even though I don't agree with what John did, I can see him doing it. He always felt unloved by Dad, even though that wasn't the case. Dad just operated with tough love, while Mom operated with a soft touch. John wasn't one who accepted criticism, whether constructive or not.

Countless times Mom told me that she and Dad did not give up on John. She believed him every time he said it was the last time that he would get drunk. She loved him, even when he was in the wrong, and she tried to carry his burden for him. She was still longing for her sober son, who was kind, compassionate, and fun. She clung to the memories of the family gatherings when he wasn't drinking.

Dad didn't give up on him either, even if it looked that way to Mom. He had a different way of handling John, and that was with strict demands and high expectations. He wanted nothing more than for John to change. Unfortunately, neither of their versions worked.

CHAPTER 4

The Circle of Support

*The family served as a haven and reprieve from
the outside world for all of them.*

The consistent roller coaster of loving someone addicted to alcohol is relentless. It leaves you feeling incapable and unhelpful. You're always second-guessing yourself and your actions. The same can be said for the person dealing with the addiction. They often feel unworthy or unlovable, or they feel like any choice they make is always wrong. How do you bridge the gap between the two? How can you help someone who wants the help but struggles to receive it?

I do believe family and support systems are instrumental to a happy and productive life. Yes, you can conquer the world without them, but having them present does make it easier. Fortunately, like many others in the coalfields, our family grew up with a sense of connection and support that withstood all else. As the family's matriarch, Grandma Sparks led by example. She stood by her family in right or wrong and expected the rest of the family to fall into line. That didn't mean they received a pass for bad behavior or decisions. It just meant that she expected the family to stick together.

When Grandma's eldest daughter died from cancer, Grandma adopted her daughter's four young children and raised them as her own. With the vast age difference between children and grandchildren, the family lines were slightly blurred. The four younger kids were cared for by Grandma and their older siblings, including my mom. Mom looked after the kids since they were babies and, in some ways, felt like they were her children. She maintained a close, nurturing relationship with them after William and John were born, hence the close bond the kids shared. John and Donna's instant connection traversed adulthood.

Grandma Sparks had nine children, including the four grandchildren she adopted, and more grandkids and great-grandkids than I can remember. When John was growing up, all of them convened at Grandma's house. The adults would hover on the porch or around the fire talking as the grandkids ran through the mountains playing or singing. Yes, you read that correctly; several of them enjoyed singing. I'm not saying they were great, but they knew how to have fun together. The kids also grew up under the guidance of one of the best pranksters in the county, Uncle LJ. He often enjoyed picking on the kids and Grandma, which usually resulted in laughs and scolding.

Those times together are how Donna and John became so close. As teenagers, he felt the need to serve as her protector anytime a guy broke her heart. He was the first person to step up to fight for her, even if it was a fight that he may lose. Luckily Donna didn't allow it to go that far. Even though she intervened, John still spoke his piece in a not-so-nice, matter-of-fact way so that the man knew he was wrong.

My parents and John found strength in the family bonds that Grandma Sparks had instilled. The family served as a haven and reprieve from the outside world for all of them. The world didn't always treat Mom or John kindly. There were some who reveled in John's mistakes and took every opportunity to share them with anyone who listened. Small-town living was not conducive to privacy. Therefore, acquaintances often called Mom to inform her about John's latest antics, either out of genuine concern or as an assertion of their "better-than-you" attitudes. That's the good and bad of a small community; some people are friends, some are not, but they all know everything about you.

As an adult, it breaks my heart to think of how she must have felt during those phone conversations. How do you listen to others talk negatively about your son, especially knowing that it was probably true? She couldn't justify his actions, so instead, she had to just listen quietly. I wonder if she was able to conceal her tears or if the person on the other end heard them.

I am grateful that for every foe, there was a stronger friend or family member there for Mom and John. They may have faced negativity, but they didn't face it alone, even if it felt that way. Mom pulled away from others and buried her feelings deep inside, not allowing people to see the despair that she was in. The walls she constructed around certain areas of her life left her lonely. The thought of discussing John with others made his actions more real.

Acknowledging his faults brought them into the light. By tucking them away in a small room of her heart, she could avoid that subject and the pain that came with it. The dark circles and bags that hung below her eyes were never mentioned. The reason she operated in a sense of exhaustion was unspoken. Friends and family knew, but they didn't bridge the conversation.

For me, I feel better having friends to talk with when things go awry in my life. Being able to unload the stress from my mind into spoken words lightens my load. I can't imagine how the worry and stress ate at Mom from the inside. Did she want to scream at the top of her lungs for help or sink away into a deep hole?

Not sharing your true self with others leaves a void and longing for connection that increases stress and depression. In so many ways, she felt alone and carried a burden too heavy for one person, but to protect her son, she carried it without complaint. I don't know how she was able to push all of that down and still function with a smile, but she did. Mom allowed very few people to see the vulnerable side of her, the side that cried after dark and felt lost in her own house.

The same could be said for John. He didn't share his disappointment or pain with others until it was at a boiling point. He didn't open up about what bothered him, instead he used alcohol as an outlet. Both coping with different mechanisms still brought unintentional pain to themselves.

John and Mom had one confidant in common, Donna. Donna was someone whom John turned to when he couldn't go home to Mom. Instead of judging him, Donna just listened. He felt a kindred connection to her that allowed him to share all his thoughts and ridiculous ideas. Aunt Donna was a nurturer by nature, so instead of being the disciplinarian, she tried to be the understanding person he could always turn to.

She knew his behavior sober and drunk well enough to know that lashing out at him while he was drinking would only do more harm than good. One of two situations would happen: He would storm off in a fit of rage and drive while drunk, or he would lash out at her. Neither was a good option, so she placated him to keep him there, calm and safe, until he was sober. I'm not a doctor or a counselor, but to me, her way of dealing with John was smart. She may have given him the belief that she didn't consider his drinking as horrible as other family members did, but she kept him and others safe.

Due to their conversation, he would usually leave there a little calmer than he had come. Donna was quite the opposite when he left. She knew her sister worried about John, and sharing his latest visit would only increase the worry. Donna was tormented by deciding what secrets to keep and which to share with her sister. In a sense, she was the rope in tug-of-war.

John's circle was growing and evolving based off the state of his life. Donna and Mom were both drawn into each group by association. One of those associations led to a lifelong friendship and a baby girl.

CHAPTER 5
Snowy Arrival

The irony of my name is not lost on me. Was
I named after a liquor and a singer?

The details of how and when my birth mother and birth father started dating are vague at best. My birth mother, Karen, a young widow left to care for a baby boy alone, took shelter with her older brother, Paul, and his wife, Sherry. The unexpected goodbye to the husband she loved and the life she had dreamed of left her sleep deprived and emotionally exhausted. Coping with her new reality, she found solace in alcohol, drinking to cover the heartache and loneliness that were leaving her eyes void of laughter and her slender lips curved down.

Destiny or proximity placed Karen and John on a singular path that consumed them both. Living mere minutes from one another, he drove past Karen's house every day. Drawn to Paul and Sherry's either by the camaraderie or by the pretty lady in the yard, John became a frequent visitor. Both dealing with their own demons, they were drawn to one another. Looks may not have been the primary connection, but they were part of the spark. Karen's slender build, long straight dark hair, and thin smile were captivating. John's six-foot slender frame and booming voice demanded attention when he walked into a room. His wavy brown hair and thin smile kept a woman's attention.

Going past their looks, a deeper connection formed through the mutual love of David, Karen's son. He was a blond-headed, fair-skinned little boy who had the biggest smile and puffy cheeks. He was a talker from the time he realized how to make sounds. John loved him and considered him a son. Not only did John love Karen and David, but his parents did as well. Mom and Karen formed a special bond that others may not have understood. Mom enjoyed her company and conversation. Mom was also hopeful that John had met his match, someone who could exist in his world while still standing up to him when he was wrong.

At some point Karen moved from Paul's home to her own trailer across the road. I don't believe she and John officially lived together, even though he did spend a lot of time there. I have speculated that no longer having an audience allowed both to drop their guard and not be on their best behavior. It's easy to allow the darker side of you to show when others aren't watching.

Their romantic relationship slowly devolved into a cycle of alcohol and partying that led to fights and anger. Over the time span of five years, there were fights, breakups, and make-ups that kept both on a roller coaster. I was conceived during the tumultuous time of their relationship—a surprise baby that neither of them had planned for or wanted.

The only birth story I know has been recounted to me several times by Mom and her sister, Donna. Mom rambled through laughter, "John stumbled over his own feet running out the door and down the three wooden steps to clear the snow pile surrounding the truck. Slipping and sliding on the packed-down snow, John started pulling his silver chains out from behind the truck seat. He darted from wheel to wheel jacking up each one individually to securely wrap the chain around the tire, hoping the chains would provide extra traction for the drive to Whitesburg Hospital."

Karen yelled at him, "Hurry up before I give birth in the damn house!"

Squinting his eyes and hissing back at her, he said, "Give me a damn minute." Then he walked by her and called Mom.

Mom couldn't say hello before he yelled, "I can't do this shit."

In the background Karen hollered, "Joyce, your grandbaby is going to be born in this house if John doesn't get his ass out there and finish cleaning off the truck."

Trying to deescalate the situation, Mom told John that he needed to calm down and focus on what had to be done to get Karen and me to the hospital safely. She laughed as she said that the phrase "calm down" only enraged him more.

He started yelling, "Calm down! How the hell do I calm down? Since you have all the answers, you just take them to the hospital."

I cut in and asked, "Was John angry at Karen or me?"

"No, he wasn't angry; he was scared. His fear often showed in anger," Mom responded.

The drive to the hospital was longer than normal, but they made it safely without Karen giving birth on the side of the road. With the snowy weather and unplanned labor, I do not know if anyone made it to the hospital on the day I was born. There are no pictures from the hospital that document my time there. I hope that John was in the delivery room with Karen, but again, I can't say for certain either way. No woman should be alone on such a momentous day.

On February 18, 1979, my birth certificate read Brandi Dawn Dishman—my birth mother's last name—not Isaac. I was not given my birth father's name, either by his choice or lack of choice. The reason behind my last name was never explained to me. Instead, I saw it on my pediatric health chart years later. A black marker had drawn a single line through "Dishman" and written "Isaac" beside it. In a stroke of a marker, the last name that connected me to my birth mother was replaced with the name that connected me to my new parents.

Curious about how John and Karen settled on my first and middle name, I asked the only person I could, Mom. She didn't know who chose Brandi or why—it had never occurred to her to ask either of them. My middle name was chosen on the way to the hospital. A singer or song that came on the radio sparked the inspiration for Dawn.

The irony of my name is not lost on me. Was I named after a liquor and a singer?

To appease my curiosity, I Googled "Dawn 1979," and there was indeed a backup singer for Tony Orlando named Dawn and a song titled "Dawn" by Frankie Valli and the Four Seasons that was released in 1964. Maybe there is some truth to the story. Either way, it's the only story I have of Karen and John preparing for my birth. So, I hold on to it and smile because in true fashion the reasoning behind the name fits their personalities.

If documentation was required for proof of birth, it would be as if I didn't exist. There wasn't a scrapbook lovingly prepared to memorialize my milestones, such as my birth, weight, and height. There isn't a silly picture of the three of us together smiling for the camera. There isn't a picture of me being cleaned up after birth or stretched out in the crib to be measured. The only keepsake from the day I was born was a birth certificate issued by the state, and that is now gone as well. That birth certificate was replaced with the one I use today, the one with the last name Isaac.

There was no special bring-home outfit placed in a keepsake trunk and no baby blanket that I carried until it fell apart—just a man, woman, and baby. Coming home wasn't a big deal. I wonder if there were any balloons or stuffed animals sent to the hospital to wish Karen and me well. Did family gather around to see us? Were meals lovingly prepared for us after arriving home? I wonder how she fared after my birth. Did someone help her? Was someone there with her, or did she shoulder it alone? There are so many questions that I do not and will not have answers to.

After being discharged from the hospital, Karen and I returned home to her singlewide trailer, where David was waiting for us. With the proximity of Karen's trailer, it was easy for John to visit as often and spontaneously as he liked, which I am sure wasn't always optimal. From Mom's vague recount, Karen, David, and I moved in with her and Dad because John claimed I wasn't being properly cared for. Supposedly, I was found between the wall and mattress in the back bedroom. I don't know how that could be true for a newborn, but nevertheless John stuck to it. Even though John didn't want the responsibility of being a full-time parent, he was overly critical of Karen, or maybe he was rightfully critical. Either way, Karen gave in to his request or demand and moved into his childhood home with his parents, soon to be mine.

Within a matter of a few days, Mom and Dad went from a partially empty nest to a full house. The number of people to care for multiplied from three to six without my parents complaining. Karen could have taken over an open bedroom, but for whatever reason, she chose to sleep on the couch with me, which couldn't have been comfortable. But thinking of my own early days with my newborn kids, I realize that I slept on the couch a lot as well. So, maybe it was just a mom thing.

Within the first three weeks of my life, my grandparents transitioned to Mom and Dad. I was no longer a guest but a permanent resident of their home. For the next 18 years, they were solely responsible for me. Mom or Dad rocked me to sleep at night. They consoled me when I cried. When I was sick, they paced the floor, wringing their hands with worry. They were and will always be my parents. Mom and Dad chose me. With them, I had security and love that I will forever be grateful for.

Adjusting to a newborn in the house permanently is vastly different from one visiting. Changes and concessions were made to accommodate me and all the things that I needed. The downstairs bedroom was converted to my makeshift nursery. Along one side of the room was a full-size bed with a crib placed along the wall in front of it. Mom slept downstairs with me while Dad slept upstairs. His early-morning work schedule didn't allow for a crying baby waking him up through the night. My crib being downstairs also made it easier for Mom to carry out her daily chores without running up and down the steps to check on me during nap time.

With Mom and Dad both adjusting to being parents to a baby once again, Karen transitioned out of the home. With the adoption decided, I assume it was easier for all to have a complete break, that way responsibilities and boundaries were set. I wonder how she felt as a mother leaving one of her children behind. Was she heartbroken or relieved? Did she regret her decision? I don't know if she and John still dated after she moved out. Again, another question that I didn't ask.

CHAPTER 6
Unbreakable Cycle

Within a few short months, he lost his freedom and the title of father. Was that too much to lose?

Routines and boundaries were being established between the adults as I lay blissfully unaware of all the stress around me. After Karen moved out, John continued to live with our parents, which meant he was still present and active in my daily life. His wild side had not been tamed by my birth. He continued to drink and party as he pleased. His reckless behavior reached a climax that our parents were not able to undo. Therefore, he faced the consequences that no one wanted.

In the late winter or early spring of 1979—months after I was born—John and a small group of friends were out drinking when an altercation ensued between him and another man. Caution and restraint were not exercised while drinking. Once enraged, he couldn't be calmed down easily—very few people had mastered that trait. Unfortunately, none of them was there to change the trajectory of his anger.

The fight between John and an unnamed man occurred for reasons unknown to me today. Witnesses were unable to break up the fight, and John wasn't able to escape before the police arrived on the scene. The officers immediately intervened and broke up the fight before anyone was hurt badly. Due to John being drunk in public and fighting, the officers had the right to search his vehicle.

Stored in the trunk was a sawed-off shotgun. Now, he didn't have it out or threaten to use it, but that was insignificant. He was arrested and charged with being in possession of an unregistered firearm while intoxicated and with disorderly conduct. The severity of the charges meant prison time was inescapable for John.

Again, my parents longed for the time in prison to not be in vain. It was a period of grief but also of opportunity. Acknowledging a positive perspective in a heartbreaking reality, Mom recounted to me that if time away would help him eradicate his alcohol dependency, the stint would have been worth it. Mom and Dad lost countless nights of sleep and cried silent tears as John served out his sentence. Even though the consequences of his actions were justifiable, the worry for his well-being was at the forefront of their mind.

My parents reluctantly accepted that John would be transported to a distant prison with unknown guards or employees to ease the transition. Leaving the county jail, he would be cuffed and escorted into a prison van and dropped off inside of a tall, heavily guarded fence. His meals would be placed on small plastic or metal trays at designated times without concern for food preferences. There would not be a soft bed to lay his head on; instead he'd have a prison cot with meager linens. Since John wasn't allowed to use the phone or receive visitors freely, Mom waited by the phone for the chance to hear his voice. The distance between the prison and our home limited our ability to visit.

When I was only a few months old Granny Martha, Mom, and I traveled to the prison to visit John. Granny Martha, not family by blood but by spirit and love, had been by Mom's side for years. Mom and Martha had become friends when Mom and Dad were newlyweds. Their friendship spanned births, child-rearing, empty nests, and deaths. She was a rock that Mom poured her heart out to, without fear of betrayal. Granny Martha was the friend who always showed up with unconditional love when someone needed her. She was my first example of what a true friend should be like.

Mom shared with me that John's eyes and demeanor had changed to a defeated man. His shoulders were slumped with his head bowed down. He no longer made eye contact or even slightly raised his head. With his head tilted down, his eyes were hard to see. The only prominent attribute was the darkness that encircled them. His voice was low, and he spoke slowly without emotion. He was solemn with a forced grin.

I can reconstruct John's appearance with an eerily accurate recount of Mom's description, which is hard to align with the John I knew. The John I was familiar with was loud, rambunctious, and fearless. What is harder about that conversation is recalling how Mom looked and sounded while talking about John. Grief took the life out of her. Have you talked with someone struggling with grief? Their voices are different. There was no animation in her voice, only a monotone. Her face drooped into a permanent frown when we talked about John and his alcoholism.

The prison visit was one of finality. Mom visited her son in prison to discuss the last phase of my adoption. She had to level another blow to his already beaten self-confidence by discussing the legality of signing over his only child at the time. As John sat in prison, losing all that was important to him, was this adoption truly what he wanted?

The adoption had been decided when John had the world at his feet, coming and going as he pleased with no responsibilities and no one to interrupt his life. Now that everything had changed and he was alone, did he regret his decision? Did he wish that he had handled things differently? Or was he relieved? Within a few short months, he lost his freedom and the title of father. Was that too much to lose? Was that the point of no return?

My chest aches when I think about my birth father sitting in prison alone, possibly frightened and lonely. I still bite my bottom lip to keep the tears from flowing for him and my parents when I think of that confusing time. I'm grateful that I have no memory of the prison visit. I hope that my presence helped ease Mom and Dad's pain and worry. If anything, I hope I was a distraction to the chaos that was circling John's life.

Once released from prison in the early '80s, he stayed with us for a little while. I was the sole recipient of his attention, if only briefly. Sitting on the couch and leaning back, he would cuddle with me as he watched TV, often taking breaks to play with me on the floor. Mom said he was a great babysitter till it was time to change my diaper, then he was hunting for her.

Unfortunately, his contentment started to waver, and he missed the excitement of his previous life. Feeling the need to be alive again, he started going out in the evenings. The time that he was home started to lessen until he was gone more than he was there. The excuses started to dissipate until he no longer offered a reason. He just left, sometimes staying gone all night, which was often better than him coming home still drunk.

On the occasions when he would stumble in still half-drunk, he was usually looking for an argument, and he didn't care whom it was with. Mom said that during those episodes, she tried to appease him or avoid any mention of something that would further upset him. Sometimes, that wasn't possible. On one such occasion, his anger was geared toward me.

Blissfully unaware, I was asleep in my crib, snuggling with a new doll that William had bought me. Without regard to me, John stomped through my nursery to use the bathroom. The only bathroom downstairs was attached to my nursery, so I grew accustomed to walk-throughs and began to sleep through most of them. Glancing over at me in the crib, he noticed the new doll.

Either upset, jealous, or both, he woke me with his roaring voice, yelling, "Who got her this new doll?"

Mom scampered into the bedroom, whispering, "Shh, shh, John, she was asleep. The doll is from William."

Jealously paired with alcohol caused him to begin yelling. "Why the hell did he get it for her? She don't need any more dolls." His screaming paired with my crying was enough to be heard throughout the house. Without hesitation he pulled his pocketknife from his jeans and flipped open the blade.

Mom started stuttering, "John, no! John, no!"

He stood there contemplating where to stab the doll first when Dad charged through the dining room. "Son, that's enough. You will not scare that baby in my house," he barked.

John, still standing between Dad and me, paused for a minute, looking between us before his attention turned to Dad.

John's singular step toward Dad caused Mom to panic. "John, no, he's your father!" she screamed.

Dad, unafraid, said, "Joyce, get Brandi. John, let's take it to the porch."

I don't know what happened on the porch that evening, if John backed down or Dad. I don't know if there were more hurtful words exchanged or any physical altercation. All I know is that Dad protected me. He put himself at the forefront of John's anger and took it away from where I was.

I think of that time frame, me lying there as a child, crying and screaming because I knew something was wrong. I may not have understood the words, but the vibes and tones were enough for me to react to. Listening to that story as an adult is difficult for me. Accepting that my birth father was so jealous that he would have stabbed a doll that I was holding hurts me. His mom, dad, and brother were filling the voids that he left behind. He chose to only be an occasional parent to me. Why should he be angry when someone else gave me a small gift?

The hurt I feel for what he did to me does not compare to the pain I feel over how he hurt Mom and Dad that day. Standing in their home, they had to choose one child over another. To protect one, they had to stand against the other. Putting them in a situation of potential violence was unfair and unnecessary.

Even when Dad was tired, he served as the strong force against John. Dad was a man who stood up for what was right even against his own blood. I'm not saying that it made it easy on him, because it didn't. He didn't like taking a hard stand with any of us. He preferred to be the supporter, not the enforcer.

Mom and Dad knew John had reverted to his old ways but were at a loss on how to intervene and change his direction. Every approach they had tried failed miserably, whether it was tough love, begging, or negotiating. Here was a man who had nothing more to lose. He had a criminal record, an alcohol dependency, and he had lost custody of his only child. He took on the world with no concern for the outcome.

Realizing that his lifestyle was not going to be tolerated or accepted, he moved out. I'm not sure where he lived during that time span, but I know it was close—close enough that he visited us almost daily. He and Mom would sit around the kitchen table talking for hours. John shared everything with Mom, even things she would have preferred not to hear.

Now that John was living on his own, money was tighter for him, so he often had to borrow from Mom. When he walked into the house with his head down and shoulders slumped, Mom knew he needed something. He would usually pull out the kitchen chair, face the window, and light an unfiltered Camel cigarette. Mom would pull out the seat across from him and sit down to listen. When I was older, she would ask me to go play in the living room. I'm not sure why she sent me in there since I could still hear almost everything.

After I was out of sight, she would ask John what was wrong. His reply always began in a similar fashion, a financial hardship that hit unexpectedly. His stories usually revolved around offering excuses of why he was out of cash and needed more, but he always emphasized that it was not alcohol related. Mom knew better. I knew better too.

She would just sit there, quietly listening to him explain why his money was tight, then she would ask, "John how much do you need?"

He responded, "Mom, I promise I will pay you back when I get my next check."

The amount was never the same, but the answer was always yes. In fact, she had a small pink-and-black trinket bowl in the top of one of our kitchen cabinets that served as a revolving door of money for John. She was accustomed to him asking for money on week two of his paycheck, so she kept cash in the trinket bowl for him.

On payday he often walked through the back door with his black leather Harley-Davidson chain wallet in his hand, wasting no time paying Mom back for the money he had borrowed the week before. With almost a sense of pride, he would count out the bills on the kitchen table before gathering them up and placing them in Mom's hand.

The necessity of always repaying his debts and being a man of his word are positive attribute that he gleaned from his parents. He had a lot of good traits that alcohol couldn't stifle, even if he didn't see them, others did.

Before accepting the money, Mom would always ask John if he needed it. I can still hear her say, "Now, I don't need that money. If you do, keep it."

I don't recall John ever keeping the money. She placed the money in the pink-and-black trinket bowl for safekeeping. So, when the request for money came again, as it often did, she had it available.

CHAPTER 7
Love Exists

She knew one day that I would want—no, need—
those positive memories to feel complete.

John rotated through several different friend groups, some of them social drinkers, some other alcoholics like him, and some who were considered good ole boys. John and Karen had not been in a relationship for a while but still saw each other on occasion. On one such evening, John and Karen had been together, I assume, drinking. For some unbeknownst reason, John was angry at Mom.

Mom had just picked me up in the living room and was carrying me to the kitchen for dinner when Karen came barging through the front door, yelling, "Joyce, are you okay?" startling me and Mom at the sudden commotion.

Karen was gasping for breath, and her words were difficult to understand as she bent over to take some deep breaths. "John's mad, coming here," is what Mom was able to understand before the heavy wooden back door slammed into the wall and John's loud boots stomped through the kitchen.

Slinging his arms and widening his stride, John approached Mom with fierceness in his eyes. Her arms tightened around the three-year-old me, and her body stiffened, fearing the confrontation. In an instant, Karen pushed Mom aside and stepped in front of us. With adrenaline still coursing through her body, she said, "You will have to go through me before you get to Joyce or Brandi."

His red face and beady eyes glared at Karen with intense anger. Unwavering in her determination to protect us, she stared stone-faced at him without an inclination to back down. Glaring at her, John warned, "Karen, you will pay for this."

"I'm ready for you," she responded.

"That's enough, both of you," Mom yelled. "John, I don't know what your problem is, but this is no way to fix it. Sit down and talk to me."

Angry at both women, John turned to exit through the kitchen, taking his left arm and swatting items off the countertop. He shouted without looking back, "Forget both of you, forget it all." Slam! The back door closed behind him, shaking the pictures on the wall.

I asked Mom what I was doing during the confrontation, because I was too young to remember.

She paused for a few seconds before admitting that she wasn't sure. "When I looked over at you, you had a vacant stare on your face, looking straight ahead. There was no real emotion on your face. That night as I got you ready for bed, you cried and asked, 'Why was John mad? Can I fix it?'"

I have no recollection of that disagreement, but I can picture it almost meticulously by the way Mom recounted it to me. I wondered for years why she shared that story with me, what the significance of that argument was. I finally realized it was for my benefit. She wanted me to know that Karen did care about me and her.

Mom had a way of always focusing on the good in John and Karen and making sure that I always saw it. She knew one day that I would want—no, need—those positive memories to feel complete. John and Mom could argue that day and be over it that evening. Neither ever held a grudge against the other. When Mom needed help or a ride, John loved coming to her rescue.

Mom did not have her driver's license and had no desire to learn. I don't know if that was because she was worried that Dad would be upset if she went too many places or if she was afraid to learn how. Maybe a little of both? I find it hard to believe that either is the full reason for not learning how to drive. She was lonely at home and often had to rework her schedule to adapt to Dad's work schedule.

With Dad working overtime plus maintaining his garden and cutting the grass, he didn't have a lot of free time to take us places, so we depended on others. When John was at home, he was often willing to help, which made it convenient.

On one of the short trips to Whitesburg, maybe a 25-minute drive depending on how fast you drove, we passed through Ermine, where a vendor on the side of the road caught my attention. Sitting there beside the road beckoning to me was a brown floral couch and matching chair that were just my size. I could tell from just driving by that it was the soft velvety material that would tickle your bare legs. Squealing like a five- or six-year-old would, excitedly slapping Mom on the arm, I hollered, "Look! Look!"

John and Mom, both in frustration, asked, "What, Brandi Dawn? What, Brandi Dawn?"

When my middle name was used, that usually meant I was in trouble—but not that day. I had just startled them. John and Mom were both looking from side to side, trying to figure out what had caused me to become so excited. Then out of his side mirror, he caught a glimpse of the vendor.

With the sudden push of the truck's brakes, Mom and I were both thrown against the dash, only to be thrown backward against the seat when John pulled the truck into reverse. We slid into the parking lot almost sideways as he stopped in front of the vendor. I didn't know if I was getting a whopping or the set, so I sat silently until a big smile spread across his face and he said, "Well, come on."

I was lying on the couch, already claiming it as mine before I was certain I would get it. I couldn't hear the conversation between him and Mom, but by the smile on his face, I knew I would like the outcome.

Walking toward me, he dropped his head and tucked his lips together, acting as if he were delivering bad news. Before he could even speak, Mom

IN BETTER HANDS: AN APPALACHIAN MEMOIR OF HEALING AND GRACE

started laughing, which caused a chain reaction in each of us. He laughed as he said, "Hell, I can't carry you and the couch."

I rolled off that couch and onto the gravel lot so fast that my hands didn't have time to catch me before I hit the ground. I jumped up and tried to help him and Mom, which only resulted in me being in the way. Both told me to move more times than I could count. Finally, I stepped back out of the way and marveled at my new living room set. It was beautiful.

Normally I loved our trips out and was never in a hurry to rush home, but that day was different. I couldn't wait to get home and place my new living room set in the back of the living room. It was the perfect addition to the baby dolls and mini nursery play area I had. This living room set was the final touch to make my little area feel like a true home.

With it loaded in the back of his old truck, I continually turned around to admire my beautiful new living room set. Every time I turned around, I would nudge either Mom or John, which started to annoy them. They both kept telling me to turn around, that I was going to hurt my neck, but I didn't care. I was so excited that nothing could have bothered me.

I don't know if it was Mom or John who paid for the living room set. I always assumed it was John because he was so proud of it. I can still see his smile while he was loading it in the truck. Now I wonder if he was proud of himself for being able to give me something that I so wanted. Had he always felt as if he let me down and wasn't able to do things for me as others did? I hope he didn't feel that way, because material objects weren't important to me, then or now. I wish I could have told him that. I didn't need gifts from him, just his attention. I wonder if then he would have realized he was enough.

CHAPTER 8

The Man We Loved

He was so much more than his addiction.

Many of my stories and memories of John revolve around alcohol. The good times we shared were overshadowed by the painful memories of his drinking. I buried the anger and animosity festering in my heart so that others wouldn't see my true feelings. Allowing others to know I was upset with him seemed like a betrayal to him and my parents. I felt a need to protect him to my own detriment.

The anger didn't diminish the love I had for him. I still loved him just as much as always. I instinctively pounced to his defense every time someone uttered a mean word about him. It's a battle that doesn't make sense—one that you cannot fully comprehend unless you love an addict. It's a confusing mindset because you love one person who can behave two different ways.

I would be doing John's memory an injustice by portraying a unilateral narrative of him. He was indeed multifaceted—a son, father, friend, and struggling addict. I feel those varied personas' internal battles were difficult for him to regulate and react to accordingly, often leaving him turning to alcohol for relief. The sober John, the larger-than-life man invincible to all, is whom I try to think of now. He was the man who brushed his hair from his face as he pushed me on the swing for the hundredth time, the man who stood in the high school parking lot as I rode circles around him on my new bike.

He was so much more than his addiction. He was the man who took me pretend fishing, the man who took me on picnics. He was the man who cried at the kitchen table over Grandma Isaac, the man whose laugh could fill a room. Alcohol may have changed him, but it will never replace the good part of him.

John, Mom, and I were out on yet another shopping adventure that brought us to Dawahare's. Most of my holiday outfits and fancy dresses came from Dawahare's during my younger years. The reason behind our shopping trip is unknown to me—maybe I asked to look at something, or Mom was looking for a special outfit, I don't remember.

The Dawahare's sign shone brightly in the middle of downtown Neon. The beautiful angled-glass entry with the large awning appeared regal and luxurious. Behind the windows, the bright lights and precision layout of the store racks invited you in. Before entering the store, the scent of perfume and new merchandise rushed out to welcome you on the street. Inhaling the scent combination, I knew this must be how women should always smell. Walking through the door, you were greeted with a "Hello, how may we help you today?" It didn't matter if you were only browsing or buying; everyone was addressed.

On each clothing rack, items were color-coordinated and spaced perfectly apart. Coordinating outfits were grouped together, and mannequins were styled for inspiration. It was a treat to look at the clothes, never mind trying them on and buying them. During this particular shopping trip, I saw a fur coat I wanted more than anything.

It was the middle of the summer, and I was not leaving the store without it. Mom drew a hard line on purchasing the coat—even though it was on sale, the likelihood of it fitting me during the winter or the need I would have for it didn't justify the cost.

John couldn't stand hearing Mom tell me no while I was begging. So, he purchased the coat for me. Standing in the store, I slid my arms into that thick fur coat and walked proudly out the front door into the summer heat. Paying no mind to the sweat on my face and body, I wore the coat until we were home. It wasn't until I started to feel sick that I removed the coat and laid it on my play sofa.

I think of that purchase and wonder if John had the extra money to buy that coat or if he did without to give it to me. Was the reason he needed money from Mom because he purchased items for me that I didn't need? Maybe it wasn't always due to alcohol. I don't believe he bought that coat to shut me up. I believe he purchased it because it made him proud—he was giving me something I wanted, something that no one else would buy.

When I was young, eating fast food was a treat, not something that I asked for or expected regularly. During the heat of the summer, Dad worked countless hours tending to the garden or gardens, sometimes responsible for three gardens at once. Once the winter weather broke, he was in the garden with his blue work pants and light-blue long-sleeved button-up shirt, pushing the tiller in perfectly spaced rows. Tilling the ground left soft mounds of dirt ready for seeds or sprouts to be planted.

The work didn't stop once the vegetables were in the ground—that was when the work began. Dad checked the garden weekly, pulling weeds, hoeing the dirt, and watering the crops if necessary. It seemed as if harvest time came all at once, leaving little time to pick and preserve the vegetables before they were rotten. Dad and William would spend days in the garden gathering the vegetables in gallon buckets that were carried into Mom. Old sheets would be laid across the kitchen, dining room table, and portions of the floor for the vegetables to be spread out. We couldn't risk the vegetables sweating, so adequate airflow was necessary.

Our kitchen and dining room resembled a farmers' market, with heaps of vegetables laid out. Mom worked for hours breaking beans, shucking corn, boiling tomatoes, and sorting cucumbers for pickling. The canned food—pickled corn, mixed pickles, sauerkraut, and dill pickles—were placed in glass jars, then sealed and stacked in the cool basement. Sweet corn, beans, peppers, and tomatoes were sealed in freezer bags and stacked in the freezer according to the date. That amount of food lasted through the winter and beyond. I loved pickled foods, basically eating them out of the jar when allowed. Mom was an excellent cook. She could take a few random items and create a yummy meal.

On the off chance that she was fixing something I didn't like, she would always prepare something different for me, even if I didn't ask. Often Mom would prepare two separate meals without a fuss or complaint—truly just a loving heart. With all the food we had stored in the house, eating out seemed like a waste and maybe an insult to the hard work that Mom and Dad put into growing and preserving the food.

Rarely eating out made it more of a special treat for all of us. Dad was at work one afternoon, so it was just me, Mom, and John at the house. He offered to take us to Hardee's in Jenkins for dinner. I was secretly hoping that Mom would say yes—well, as secretly as you could be by saying, "Please, Mom," with a huge smile. Not giving her time to answer, I danced around, begging her to say yes. Finally, through my constant pleading, she agreed. I don't know how I even heard her, considering I was talking nonstop. Completely disregarding Mom telling me to brush my hair or change clothes, I was already walking toward the back door.

John's pale-yellow Chrysler was backed down our curvy driveway, so only a few steps stood between me and a break from the monotony. Even if that outing was only to Jenkins, maybe a 15-minute drive each way, it was like a mini vacation to me. I didn't give Mom time to push the front seat forward before I tried to wedge myself into the back seat. By the time Mom had figured out how to pull the front seat to the dash, I was halfway in. She and John both laughed at my excitement to go to Hardee's.

Mom wouldn't have admitted it then, but I believe she was also excited to be out. It was a lonely life, just her and me in the house, with no way to go anywhere without depending on someone else to take us. Dad wasn't one who believed in keeping the roads hot or wasting money on gas, so we only went out of necessity.

Standing at the Hardee's counter, I had no idea what to order, but I finally settled on chicken with one of every dipping sauce. Not wanting the outing to end (I assume), John suggested we go to Fishpond Lake for a picnic. The lake was just a few minutes from Hardee's and could techni-cally be considered on the way home.

I once again applied pressure. "Mom, please, can we go? Please, Mom, I don't want to go home."

She turned around in the seat, looking at me, smiling, and almost laughing at my excitement. She rolled her eyes in the way of being silly, not annoyed, and agreed.

We crept around the lake, stopping at every picnic area to see if it was utilized until we found a vacant site. When John pulled off the pavement and onto a small gravel road that faced the water, my heart started racing. The fear of water and drowning was rushing through my mind. I started wondering, what if the brakes go out? What if we slide into the water? My thoughts didn't slow until we were safely parked facing the water. The lake was quiet, and the sun reflected off the water, giving us a beautiful view for dinner.

Mom lowered the armrest between her and John for me to climb into the front seat with them. They placed each of my open sauces on the dash-board for me to try. Trying honey mustard and sweet-and-sour sauce for the first time on chicken, I loved them both. After taking a few bites, I turned to Mom and asked, "Can you make these sauces at home?"

She laughed and said, "I will try."

I took my time eating my dinner. I wanted to savor this moment for as long as I could. There was no arguing or drinking—just laughter, some-thing our family needed more of.

Had John only seen the man that we saw—the man behind the alco-hol, the one who was loved and missed, the man whom we all wanted in our lives—would that have saved him?

CHAPTER 9
Stark Difference

Every time he visited, I didn't know which John I was getting,
the sober John I loved, or the alcoholic John whom I feared.

I had a serious toy problem that my entire family fed into. The back of the large rectangle living room was overrun with baby dolls, pretend house furniture, and Barbies. I'm not sure how I even fit back there to play. It was jokingly said that our living room could have been the Barbie aisle at Walmart. Practically every type of toy was strewn across the floor.

Mom didn't enforce that I only use the back portion of the living room for toys, so I carried them all over the house. While watching *She-Ra* on the television, I propped up a few dolls on the couch beside me. I mean, who doesn't love cartoons, right? Bored with watching TV, I retreated to the back play area again, leaving the dolls watching TV.

John walked through the house with a cigarette in his mouth and a Pepsi in his hand. Plopping down on the couch without looking, he said, "What the hell—what's on this damn couch? Brandi, why the hell are your toys on the couch? Keep that shit over there where it belongs."

My arms shook as I shifted my weight onto them to push myself off the ground. Slowly scooting my feet along the vinyl floor, I started toward John to retrieve my dolls.

"You don't need this doll. You have more than you will ever need in that mess. Get over there and clean it up. You can't even walk in here."

My eyes widened as I turned toward Mom for guidance. Her head abruptly moved left and right, looking out of the corner of her eyes. She slowly moved her left hand backward in a wavelike motion, instructing me to sit back down behind the couch. I was adept at reading body language and tone, so I lowered back down behind the sofa without making a sound.

Bang! Bang! Bang! Three times in a row—I knew my dolls were now on the floor, their beautiful dresses possibly dirty and their perfectly styled hair a mess. I sat there surrounded by my toys with my head bowed and my arms resting in my lap, afraid to move to bring further attention to myself. That area was designated for my toys. Yes, the entire floor was covered with them, but no one else ever came to this side of the couch.

Still trying to make light of the comment, Mom laughed and said, "John, she's fine. No one walks back there but her."

He retorted, "You wouldn't have let us make that mess."

Mom didn't reengage. She knew when to leave the subject be. With no one to continue the argument with, John made his way to the front porch, and the disagreement was forgotten when he returned.

Sober John was spoiling me with gifts and clothes. Some of the same toys he was complaining about had been purchased by him. Sometimes it was okay, and others, it wasn't—it was a confusing time for me. Every time he visited, I didn't know which John I was getting, the sober John I loved or the alcoholic John whom I feared.

There was such a stark difference between the sober and drunk John that it was hard to accept he was the same man. The tactics and shenanigans that he pulled while drunk were not something he would have done sober.

In my defense, those toys were my pastime, what I did to occupy the long days of being home either alone or with my niece, Nicole. To clarify my and Nicole's relationship, I must preface that we always referred to each other as cousins instead of niece and aunt. I know that's confusing, but with only nine months between us, "niece" and "aunt" seemed weird. William and Nicole spent a lot of time at Mom and Dad's when we were younger, which allowed us to bond like sisters. We would spend hours playing with Barbies, baby dolls, and dress-up clothes.

I don't recall ever cleaning up my toys. They were what I like to refer to as an organized mess. I knew where everything was in the mountain of chaos. Mom didn't mind the mess; she was able to look over it as if it weren't even there. Dad didn't say anything either. The mess annoyed John when he was drinking, not when he was sober.

At seven years old, I lived for my Barbie dolls; they were my favorite pastime. I would sit for hours dressing them and styling their hair to get them ready for a big party that evening. They would all be dressed in their beautiful dresses, with only one date. I really needed more Ken dolls— if John laughed over my issue, I knew he was sober. While laughing, he would say there was only one Ken doll because Barbie wasn't allowed to date until she was 40.

When he started going outside for longer increments, I knew that our fun was about to come to an end. I didn't understand how he would go from the fun guy playing with me to the mean guy who scared me. His demeanor started to change—he became quieter and more distant. He would just watch TV without any interaction, no more than a grunt or nod. I knew that Mom could tell that he was changing too. She would get fidgety in her chair and look at me more frequently.

As the trips outside continued, the quietness started to fade. The sound of his voice and the look in his eyes always told the truth when he had too much to drink. He would begin to bark orders at me to quiet down so that he could hear his TV over me. He would act annoyed by the toys on the floor and say that no kid needed that much junk. That was my cue to start looking down and not make eye contact with him. I was afraid that I would do something to set him off.

In a shaky voice, Mom said, "John, I know you had a long day. Why don't you go upstairs and get some rest. I will wake you up when dinner is ready."

John's head snapped to look at Mom. "I'm fine. I don't want to lay down." Then he would start into a rolling statement of how fine he was.

The more he contested Mom, the angrier he became. He would start cussing and throwing insults, like "You don't care about me."

Mom would always respond with "Now, John, you know better." She sounded defeated with every exchange.

Who was home determined how the rest of the argument went. If Dad was home, he would come out of his man cave (a.k.a. the CB room) in a fury, saying, "Now, son, that's enough! You're not going to talk to your mother like that!" I can hear my dad's voice saying that now as plainly as I could then.

John would then turn his focus on arguing with Dad while Mom shuffled me out of the room. The arguments were always the same: cussing, idle threats, and a slammed door.

CHAPTER 10
Reconciling the Good and the Bad

*The good and bad memories often overlap, sometimes
on the same day or a few days apart.*

During the next few years, John spiraled out of control. His anger and sadness escalated to new levels. On one such night our home was filled with a fading twilight glow, and Mom's shaky voice led the way to a disastrous evening. I overheard Mom pick up the phone and flop down in her comfy chair. With a flick of the cigarette lighter and the inhalation of the first drag complete, she said, "John was in a fight," saying it low, hoping to avoid my nosy ears. "No, this one is worse. His arm or shoulder is hurt, and there is some damage to his face. No, I don't know why they were fighting. He's at the hospital now. What am I going to do with him?"

That question, "What am I going to do with him?" rattled me. Mom had the answers for everything. She was the person who seemed in control when the world was spinning out of control. She made comforting me, supporting John, and caring for Dad look easy. How could a woman who handled everything effortlessly need help? To me, she was the smartest person in the world, someone who could make any situation okay. For me, and for John, too, I believe she provided a sense of security and support—if she was there, we would be fine.

I walked back into the living room, wondering what events had unfolded that evening. What had escalated to such a degree that Mom had to call someone for help? Who would that person be? Was John okay? Who was he fighting with? I pictured scenes from movies I had caught glimpses of throughout the years. Was his face bandaged with thick white gauze? Did he need an eye patch? I had seen men wearing them. Was his shoulder okay? How did he hurt his shoulder or arm or whatever it was?

After I was sound asleep late that night, John slipped into the house and went to bed himself. Mom rose early and prepared breakfast as if it were a typical day. She didn't acknowledge the fight in front of me or talk with John where I could overhear. I didn't dare ask about the evident black eye or colorful bruises. I followed Mom's lead by ignoring John's injuries.

Years later, I learned some of the details regarding the fight. John stopped to visit someone. Maybe he was drinking? Maybe not. It was said that he provoked the fight with his rude and uncalled-for comments and actions. I don't know what the comments were or what he did. Needless to say, he lost that fight. He had a broken nose and a black eye. I don't remember a sling on his arm, but that's not to say that the doctor didn't recommend one.

More interested in who Mom turned to when she needed help than why she needed it, I asked her for the first time who her go-to person was when she could no longer hold it all.

Her face relaxed with a warm smile as she said, "My mom."

I couldn't help but tear up when I thought of my mom still going to her mom when she needed support. I thought, I hope I always have my mom to go to.

Parental instinct is to go to battle for your child, to feel this unconditional need to cocoon them away from the pain of the world, and to not allow others or even themselves to cause unnecessary pain. She was in fight mode for her son. Mom saw the sadness and consistent pain on John's face, something others couldn't see. She heard him cry to her about how unfair life was. Mom felt responsible for that unfair life and the sadness that he hid with alcohol. She broke herself doing all she could to protect him.

She didn't want the world to see him as an alcoholic who made poor decisions. She wanted them to see the sober John, who was funny and loyal. I think of the burden she carried inside, not sharing the pain with others. Watching your son battle an addiction that provoked anger and damaged his self-esteem had to be painful. The craving for him to change, the hopefulness that filled her heart each time there was a good week or even a good month. How hard it must have been to ride a roller coaster of emotions alone.

My parents tried to shield me from the chaos surrounding John, but it wasn't possible. As a kid, I was nosy and listened to the adults talk more than I should have. From those conversations, I had bits and pieces of information about John's latest escapades stored in my memory—not enough to compose a detailed story but enough to feel the sadness from recalling them. I'm grateful for that haziness. It allowed me to not fully comprehend the events that were unfolding.

The good and bad memories often overlap, sometimes on the same day or a few days apart. That's the difficult part of loving someone addicted to alcohol. Our lives resembled a seesaw—one minute, he was sober and loving, and the next, he was drinking and angry. I never knew which John would walk in the door. As a child, I quickly forgot the angry John and optimistically expected the happy John.

Several months had passed since our picnic when John asked Mom if he could take me out for an ice cream and a toy. Mom was reluctant but finally agreed after I begged her to let me go. I was around seven years old, and this was the only time I could remember being in the car with John alone. He opened the front door of his pale-yellow Chrysler, and I jumped into the front seat. The seat was so big that I was certain at least two of me could fit comfortably in it.

I sat in the middle of the seat while John pulled the tan seat belt across my body and locked it into the metal clip beside me, giving it one last pull to ensure it was tight enough before closing the door. We drove off the hill and through Neon on our way to Jenkins with the windows down and country music playing on the radio. I was dancing in the front seat, swaying as he belted out the lyrics of the songs on the radio. We laughed as our hair flew in the wind and hit our faces.

When we passed through the town of Jenkins, John said, "The drive-in has every imaginable ice cream combo you can think of. They have vanilla, chocolate, and strawberry that can be combined. Then you can pick your favorite topping: dipped chocolate, hot fudge, caramel, or strawberry."

I listened contently, then responded, "I would just like vanilla, please." Vanilla may seem plain to some people, but it was my favorite. He just shook his head and laughed in disbelief. What I found funny was that he ordered a chocolate ice cream cone. We were both similar about food. We liked certain things and didn't venture far from them. Both of us ate a particular food regularly, if not daily until we were tired of it.

Sitting on the picnic table with my feet resting on the bench, I slowly licked the top of my ice cream, allowing the sides to melt and run down my hands or drip onto my shirt. Reflexively, I ran my sticky hands through my hair repeatedly, trying to keep it out of my face. By the time the ice cream was finished, I needed a bath and a change of clothes. John didn't say a word. He just laughed as he tried to help me clean up as best we could.

He turned down the radio and looked at me as we were going through Jenkins and asked what toy I wanted from the store. I pondered for a minute and then responded maybe a Barbie, or maybe a coloring book, or maybe a baby doll. Yes, maybe a baby doll. My other dolly needed a friend.

He laughed and said, "I didn't realize dolls needed friends."

I looked at him as if he had lost it and said, "Yeah, who will they talk to when I'm not around?"

He didn't say anything else after that. I think he was trying to figure out if I thought my dolls really talked or if I was hearing voices.

A jolt of excitement hit me when John turned into the broken-up asphalt parking lot at Neon Junction. I waited impatiently for him to turn the car off, get out, and walk over to my side of the vehicle. I could have run around the car two or three times in the time it took him to open my door. Once I hopped out of the car, taking time to push my hair behind both ears, he grabbed my hand to lead me into the store. I didn't need help finding the toy section. I knew exactly where I was going. I was soon leading him.

I strolled through each toy aisle, not as much for the toys but to spend more time with him. He followed a few steps behind, offering suggestion after suggestion, even holding a couple of items I was deciding between. After thoroughly examining every row, I returned to the doll section. I looked at each one closely and picked one that looked like me. The doll had long brown hair and green eyes. I told John it was so my other doll would remember me. I didn't need another toy, but I was happy to have a new one to add to my collection.

It wasn't so much about the toys or food I enjoyed; it was being with him. I had his full attention and soaked up every minute of it. I told him that was the best day ever as we drove home. He smiled, touched my leg, and said there would be plenty more of those days.

I am embarrassed and saddened about the fact that I was nervous during that outing. Even though I relished his attention, I felt uneasy alone with John. I worried that I might say something to upset him. It was confusing for me to love someone and be scared of them at the same time. I wanted him to be the person we all needed, but as a child, I realized that wasn't possible. Instead, Mom was my safe place, and I needed her with me.

CHAPTER 11
A Child's Mistake

*Later I made the mistake of begging to attend
the celebration in front of John.*

It was the summer of 1987, and the Fourth of July celebration was fast approaching. The Neon Volunteer Fire Department worked for days prior to the festival setting up games and activities, such as ring toss, baseball throwing, color spin, duck pond, airplane rides, dunking booth, and fire truck rides. The celebration was the highlight of the summer for our small town. The football field was usually packed by late evening with families and kids screaming with excitement.

This particular year our excitement and anticipation for the celebration was overshadowed by the death of my Grandma Isaac, Dad's mom. Stress was kryptonite for John. And he was stressed—we all were—over the death of Grandma. He was looking for an opportunity to unleash his anger, and I was the target.

Grandma Isaac was my first close encounter with death, and at eight years old, I didn't fully grasp what it meant. Being told that Grandma had died and went to heaven meant nothing to me. I didn't grow up going to church regularly. I had been maybe a handful of times. Internally, I was curious why God took away people we loved. Why couldn't we all stay together forever?

I wanted to know what heaven was. Did everyone go to heaven? When do we die? So many questions filled my mind, but I felt silly not knowing.

Everyone else seemed to understand the process of death and the finality of it. So, I kept those questions to myself and listened as others talked, hoping to understand things better.

Overhearing the plans for the funeral was more unsettling. Burial plots, graves, coffins, preachers, songs, and obituaries—so many words that I hadn't heard before. I gave up trying to figure out what the adults were talking about because it seemed like a foreign language to me.

Later that day I pleaded, "Mom, can we please go to the Fourth of July celebration? Mom, the fire trucks have already started the rides through town. I know all my friends will be there. Please, Mom?"

For a young child watching from afar as others enjoyed the biggest celebration of the year in our hometown, it was a form of punishment. Pacing between the kitchen and living room, I gave real-time updates regarding crowds, parking, and the fire truck route. I didn't dare step out onto our front porch, because I knew hearing the full effect of the festival would be too much for me to handle. Weighing her options, Mom sat in the small sitting area off the kitchen, smoking a cigarette and looking out the picture window, listening to what I said but barely responding.

I put Mom in a no-win situation. Telling me no meant I was hurt and angry. Taking me may have appeared uncaring about Grandma. She was already overloaded with worry about Dad, John, and Dad's sister, Aunt Sue, and I piled more on by making her feel guilty for not taking me to the celebration.

Later I made the mistake of begging to attend the celebration in front of John. He was sitting at the kitchen table, smoking a cigarette and drinking a Pepsi while talking to Mom about Grandma. I hustled by him and into the doorway of Mom's sitting area. With my back turned to John, I asked, "Mom, can we please walk down to the celebration for a few minutes? I am so bored."

He started yelling at me. "You have no right to ask to go to that stupid thing. Grandma just died. How the hell are you bored? You have an entire damn toy store in the living room."

Startled by the anger in his voice, my chest tightened, and my arm tingled while I stood frozen in place. Breathing a little faster, I started batting my eyes to hold back the tears. I tried to tune him out, but the hateful comments were too much for me to hear. With every reiteration of how selfish I was, his voice continued to rise. I didn't turn around to look at him in fear of the anger I might have seen, so I focused on Mom.

It was one thing to hear his anger, but seeing it brought it to life. I wasn't prepared to see his face turning red and his eyebrows furrowed, so I kept my gaze on Mom and my back toward him. I waited to see if she would give me a clue on how to calm him down. After he stopped yelling at me or about me, however you look at it, I walked back into the living room and sat down to play with my toys. I needed to do something to distract me from the celebration taking place below my house and the anger that was spewing out of John.

While I was dressing my Barbies, I heard Mom say, "John, don't take it out on her. She's a kid and doesn't understand."

"Hell, she needs to know better. She can't go to that celebration," he yelled at Mom. "You should bust her ass."

"John, that's enough. Your dad doesn't need this right now. Stop taking your anger out on her," Mom retorted. She wasn't finished talking before I heard the kitchen chair scoot across the floor and slam into the table, John's boots stomp the opposite way, then the back door slam. Sighing with relief that John was gone and no more yelling would occur, I continued to play with my Barbie.

From the living room, I heard Mom walk through the kitchen and into the back bedroom. Hearing commotion in the bedroom, I got a little excited. There was a chance that she was getting ready so we could go to the celebration. I didn't get up or ask any questions. I just waited until she hollered, "Brandi, come in here and let me brush your hair."

I sprung up from the floor knowing my suspicion was right. Dad wasn't home, and Mom couldn't drive, so the only place we could have been going was to the celebration. I hurried through the dining room and into the bedroom, smiling.

"Sit down," she said with a nudge of her head.

I happily raised one leg, then the other over the antique stool and sat down in front of the mirror for her to brush my hair. Normally I complained when she brushed my hair but not that time. I kept my complaints to myself. I could handle her pulling out some tangles if it meant going to the celebration.

Feeling the sun on my face and hearing the music from the celebration, I sprinted down the hill.

Mom hollered behind me, "Slow down! You're going to get hurt."

My excitement was greater than the fear of getting hurt. I didn't pause until I was at the bottom of the hill, realizing Mom was not close.

"Brandi Dawn, don't you ever run off and leave me again. I will turn right back around and take you home." Her stern face and clinched lips worried me—I had almost lost my chance to have fun. Almost crying, I looked down at my feet and didn't speak. Laying her hand on my back, she nudged me to keep walking. Smiling at her sheepishly, I walked beside her the rest of the way.

I made a beeline to the fire truck line. To me, it was the best part of the celebration. I was so close to the fire truck that I could see the reflection of others in the red paint and the sun bouncing off the silver trim. Volunteer firefighters were gathered at the back of the truck to help riders climb up and down the metal ladder. The ladder leaning on the back of the truck was the last thing I needed to overcome for my ride to start. A little scared of its unsteadiness, I hesitated for only a second before I started climbing hand, foot, hand, foot. I paid no mind to the warm sting on my hands from touching the ladder. It was exhilarating to take the final step over the silver bar and into the back of the truck.

I would have stayed on the back of the truck the entire day if they had let me. Mom wasn't a fan of the fire truck ride, but she did it for me.

Standing in the bed of the fire truck, I scanned for the best seat still available. Finding a place on the floor, I sat down with my legs crossed as

Mom perched on the side of the truck bed. Worried I would be hurt or scared, Mom made the trek up that ladder same as I did.

Even with driving at a slow speed, the wind still whipped through my hair and across my face, and I was constantly pulling hair away from my eyes as I waved at others as we passed by. I imagined being a firefighter myself, on the way to save someone from a house fire. Our crew would pull the heavy brown hose from the top of the bed and connect it to the closest fire hydrant. Dressed in full gear, we would be unrecognizable except for the names on our coats. Running through the front door and feeling the heat from the fire, I would pick up one of the kids and rush them to safety.

This vision is the same vision I saw every time that my dad or brother went on a fire call. They were real-life heroes, running into a blazing fire to save other people. I don't know how many fires they ran into, but it is a vision that I still see today.

After riding the fire truck as much as Mom could stand, we made our way to the games. Not particularly interested in the sports games, I primarily played the "pick up a duck" game. It not only guaranteed you to win a prize every time, but it was also run by one of my favorite firemen, Tom Haynes. Tom was a jokester who always made my side hurt from laughing. I repeatedly pulled a yellow duck out of the kids' blue swimming pool and flipped it over to see the number on the bottom. The number determined which section I could pick a prize from. My loot consisted of Chinese handcuffs, little whistles, and small candies crammed into a bag to easily carry.

Bored with the games, Mom and I meandered to the food booths run by the Ladies Auxiliary. My stomach was growling for the homemade chili. A chili bun with mustard was like a five-course meal for me. Scarfing it down, I paid little mind to the chili stain around my mouth or the food that always dropped on my shirt. Finished with my real food, I was ready for dessert. Again, those ladies prepared some of the best candies, cakes, and snacks around. I filled up on everything that Mom would let me eat. Walking home, I was a little nauseated from all the food, heat, and commotion. I didn't care—it was all worth it.

The celebration concluded with a large firework display over the football field. Standing on our front porch and eating ice cream, we watched the beautiful red, blue, and green fireworks fly into the sky and erupt into a beautiful sparkle as they trailed to the ground. Oohing and awing at each display, I was amazed by the beauty. It was truly the best day of the year.

CHAPTER 12
He Loved Me

It was a fatherly act of love that, as an adult, I cherish.

Living in his own home, John had no one holding him back from drinking. I refer to it as a home, but it was more of a barn. Doorways were blocked off by thick blankets, and heat was provided by a coal stove. There were few belongings and cheap furniture. Typically, valuable items were sold or stolen for alcohol.

The prominent story from that barn, transformed into a home, is a poker game that became combative as drinking increased. Liquor and beer flowed throughout the duration of the poker game. Money was limited for most everyone at the table, so the game was only for fun. That was the plan, anyway. Toward the end of the night, the cards became harder to read, and the players' gaits were wobbly at best. They were stumbling into walls and chairs on the short walk to the bathroom. The slurred speech and incoherent comments made communication difficult.

On the way to the bathroom, one of the guys stumbled into a small table, causing it to tumble to the ground. Broken glass scattered along the floor. Amid the broken glass strewn across the floor, a picture of me lay faceup.

Angry over the broken picture frame, John jumped to his feet from the table, yelling, "Get up off the floor, you dumbass. You don't break a picture of my little girl!" He charged toward the man, as the glass cracked under his boots. The man was still sprawled out on the floor—either half-unconscious from the fall or passed out from the alcohol—so he didn't acknowledge John's comments. John straddled the man's legs, placed his weight on the guy's stomach, and drew his fist back. Pow! Pow!

"Oh, John, stop it," uttered the man on the floor.

A friend placed one arm under each of John's shoulders and pulled him off the floor. The drunk, battered man was pulled to his feet, too, which made John snarl. "Everyone get out of my damn house," he yelled.

After everyone left, John staggered to his car and drove to Aunt Donna's. Standing on her front stoop, he yelled and pounded on the door. "Donna, open this door. I know you are home." Not satisfied with the time it was taking her to open the door, he made his way around the side of the house to bang on her bedroom window.

Aunt Donna opened the door in her pajamas, with her hair a mess and eyes squinted. Paying no mind to the time or how Aunt Donna appeared, he pushed by her, entering the house. Once again, she listened until the wee hours of the morning as he complained about his life, friends, and family. By listening, Donna kept him safe. If he was talking to her, he wasn't on the road driving. So, she sacrificed her sleep to protect him. I don't know how often scenes like this took place, but I am so grateful that John had Donna to turn to when he needed someone.

John could spend the night drinking with friends and still fulfill his responsibilities the next day. I don't know how he did it because I am sure some mornings he struggled with hangovers, but he did it. When he was sober, he was also there for me and Mom, wanting to help anyway he could.

Dad had been working the early-morning shift for a while, so I had become accustomed to walking to and from school every day. The grade school was just below our hill, so it may have been a five-minute walk. I didn't mind walking in the fall or spring. A lightweight coat or sweater was enough to keep me comfortable. The winter was different for me—it was freezing. My family joked that I had no blood coursing through my veins because I was cold all the time. I complained regularly during the winter months. To me, the house was so cold, I had to get ready in front of the open oven. Again, Mom did whatever she had to, to keep me happy and comfortable, even if it wasn't necessary.

John changed shifts at the start of my third-grade year or got a new job. Either way, he worked the night shift and arrived at our house every morning before I left for school. Coming home around 7 a.m., exhausted and covered in coal dust, John went straight to the shower. I was usually starting to stir but wasn't fully awake when I heard his heavy steps as he walked through the house. That was usually Mom's sign to tell me that if I didn't get moving, I would be late for school.

John and I were both ready for breakfast around the same time—me eating pancakes or cereal and John drinking black coffee and smoking a cigarette. I sat facing the kitchen window with him seated to my right and Mom leaned up against the sink, listening as they talked. Those early-morning conversations were part of what bonded us. We were talking about nothing of grave importance, just a family having breakfast together. It felt normal and comforting.

A few minutes before it was time to leave for school, John would always go out and start his car for us. Even on the mornings that it wasn't very cold, he still did it to appease me. I didn't enjoy going to school—if truth be told, I would have rather stayed home with Mom. So, it seemed ironic that I would run from the back door to the car every morning. A cold breeze had a way of motivating me to move faster than it was, to avoid the chill. I believe that Mom and John walked slower on purpose just to annoy me, because the short walk took them a long time in my eyes.

The simple action of him staying awake after working all night, just to drive me to school, meant more than he knew. It was a fatherly act of love that, as an adult, I cherish.

CHAPTER 13
Heartbreaking Plea

*My voice was cracking from the tears, and I was gasping
for breath as I pleaded, "Please don't leave me."*

On a dreary, cold December morning, my mother woke me with a heightened sense of fear. The typical morning that consisted of our school routine had eroded due to an early-morning incident with my birth father. I was usually woken up the same way every morning, but on that morning, Mom's calm voice was replaced by tears. With her cold and shaking hand lying on my shoulder, she mumbled, "Sissy, I need you to get up and go upstairs to see John."

Like most kids, I was slow to wake up. Usually, she was patient with me as I stole a few extra minutes wrapped up in the warm covers—not that morning. Firmly she said, "Brandi, you need to get up now and go upstairs. John has been waiting on you."

Looking at my mother as I rose from the bed, I struggled to comprehend what I saw. Mom stood before me in her pajamas from the night before with disheveled hair, trying to sound strong, but her voice was cracking. Her glasses were unable to hide the redness in her eyes and the tear streaks down her cheeks. Physically shaking the image from my mind, I stood up on wobbly legs, trying to adjust my pajamas from the night before. Looking into the antique vanity mirror, I watched my shaking hand pull my shirt down over the waistband of my pajama bottoms.

I could feel my heart beating fast in my chest—it was like running during gym class, but I had only just stood up. I didn't understand these strange sensations and started to ask Mom. But when I looked at her to pose my question, I could tell now was not the right time. So, I decided to wait and ask her later after things felt normal again.

Mom was standing in the open doorway between the bedroom and dining room waiting for me to follow her. When I took my first step toward the door, she turned to lead the way to John. Following her from the bedroom to the dark dining room, I paused to see if the oven in the kitchen was on. I knew if the red light was shining and warm air was protruding from the open door, I would be getting ready for school shortly. The kitchen overhead light was on, and the chairs had been shuffled around the table, but the oven was not on.

Heated by only a coal furnace located in the basement, our home was either scorching hot or cold. If coal was not added regularly, the warm air would cool throughout the house. With everyone sleeping or at work during the night, the early-morning hours were always the coldest. So each morning during those months, I would get ready for school in front of the warm oven. Mom would sit in a kitchen chair facing the oven while I stood in front of her as she brushed my hair into a ponytail.

My uneasiness grew as I followed Mom into the dimly lit living room. I paused by the couch and listened for a sound from above that John was okay, but I was only met with silence. No doors were closing; no boots were stomping across the floor. Instead, it was as if Mom and I were the only two people in the house. I slowly followed her through the living room, pausing every few steps to allow my mind to wonder. Why was I going upstairs to see John? Why didn't he just come downstairs? The curiosity was then replaced with worry—worry about what was waiting for me at the top of the stairs. Was he hurt? Was he sick? I had no idea; all I had was my unwavering faith in Mom. John had been working the night shift for a while, so I was used to him being there in the mornings and taking me to school. It had become a new routine for us, sitting around the kitchen table and eating breakfast together.

The round table sat in the middle of the kitchen, surrounded by cabinets and appliances. The four chairs had wooden spindle backs and soft leather bottoms. Each of us settled into the same seats every morning, as if they had name tags on them. I always sat in the seat facing the window with my back to the snack cabinet. Mom sat to my left, and John to my right. Some mornings she would fix boiled eggs with pepper and coffee for him and cereal or pancakes for me. She never made breakfast for herself. She always said that eating that early made her sick, something that I couldn't comprehend. I was ready to eat as soon as my feet hit the floor every morning.

Instead, Mom always had a black ceramic coffee cup nearby filled with plain coffee—no creamer, milk, or sugar. Yuck. I didn't understand how she could drink that. It was so thick you almost needed a spoon to drink it. The family always said that Dad made the strongest coffee of anyone they knew. Well, I believe it. Mom would sit there sipping her coffee and smoking her cigarette as we ate. Our talks over breakfast were always rushed by the school bell. Mom was adamant that I be at school on time every morning. Truth be told, I hated school and would give every excuse I could to not go. Sometimes it worked; sometimes it didn't. If I was going, I was going to be on time.

When we sat around the table together, I was mostly quiet, listening to John give us a rundown of the night before. He always complained about how cold it was at the mines, how nothing ever happened there and that he just sat in his truck and looked at the orange mining gate.

Mom's rebuttal was always the same. "Well, John, it's a job."

He would huff and eat a little more of his breakfast. Since high school, John had several different jobs ranging from working for the town water department, to underground and aboveground mines, to truck mines.

Ascending the stairs with caution and slowness wasn't the norm for me, but that morning my mind was consuming all my energy. Standing on the first platform where Dad's CB room and the stairs met, I paused to look at Mom's reflection in the mirror. She didn't try to hide the tears or the fear. There was no fake smile or reassurance in her eyes. Instead, they held dread and fear. Her hand was trembling as she wiped the tears from her cheek. Mom was the strong one who held everything together. She was the one who took care of everything, but on that morning, she needed someone to take care of her. I wanted it to be me. I wanted to make the tears stop. I wanted her to be okay.

Adrenaline and fear were consuming my body, and I could no longer hide the shivering or the stutter in my voice. The effort that it required to climb up the short flight of steps left me winded. For the first time, I no longer felt safe in our home. I didn't care what was waiting for me at the top of the stairs. I didn't want to see it. I wanted to go back to bed and start the morning over.

Even as an eight-year-old, I knew that wasn't possible. I was destined to see what was waiting at the top of the stairs. There was no escaping it. With every step I climbed, my heart raced more. I was certain that Mom could see it through my shirt. It was beating so hard against my chest, it felt as if it were going to burst out. Mom's shoulders were slumped, and her head was bowed as we walked up the stairs in complete silence. Her only movement was to wipe away the tears from her cheeks.

At the top of the stairs, I was greeted by cold air seeping in around the window to my left. Out of habit I hugged my bare arms against my body to keep the warmth in and cold out. The view was almost completely obstructed by condensation, hindering a glimpse of the outside world. I knew that Mary's brown two-story home was in hearing distance of a yell. The high school was mere steps from the front door, but at the moment, they were not visible.

To my right was a shallow hallway that led to three bedrooms and a bathroom. Complete darkness overtook the back of the hallway, with the absence of the overhead light—the type of darkness that could cause a child to envision hidden monsters in the shadows. A faint light was protruding from the first bedroom on the left, so I knew John must have been in there. I slowly rotated my body and took a few steps until I was parallel with the room.

Turning my head to the right, I looked in the lit bedroom to see John sitting cross-legged against the dark-brown four-post antique bed. The back of his head was resting on the side of the mattress. His brown wavy hair was falling around his forehead into his eyes. His face looked peaked, and his smile was fake. I could tell by the way he said "Sissy" that he had been drinking. His speech was slurred but not angry this time. He was different, the calmest, most resolute that I had ever seen him. My eyes were darting around the room looking for a clue to what was happening. He wasn't sick in bed. He wasn't hurt. Why would Mom want me to see him drinking? She usually protected me from that as often as possible.

I noticed that he was adjusting himself almost as if he were trying to hide something from me. My eyes rolled to the floor, and I saw two clear bottles of liquid sitting to his left and something else sticking out from under his right leg. Later I learned the clear bottles were vodka and that the item on his right was an RG .38 caliber revolver with a two-inch barrel.

Reaching his long, slender arms out, he asked, "Can I have a hug, Sissy?"

I stood completely still, afraid to move. I could feel it in my gut that something was wrong, but I didn't know what. I was scared, but I didn't know why. I was too young to grasp what was playing out in front of me.

"It's okay, honey," Mom said, gently touching my shoulder.

I trusted my mom more than anyone else on the earth, so if she said it was okay, then it was. I slowly walked into the room, my hand grazing the antique dresser as I passed Mom.

We sat in silence, with me resting on his left leg and my head laid against his chest. His arms wrapped around me, tightly holding me against his body, and I could feel the warmth radiating off him. His soft flannel shirt was familiar as it rubbed against my arm. He was crying. Mom was crying. I was crying. I didn't know why I was crying at the time. I just knew something was wrong.

John whispered, "I love you, but I can't stay here any longer. Go back downstairs."

I sat there for a minute processing what he was saying. When I didn't rise fast enough, he nudged me gently in the back and nodded his head toward the doorway where Mom was standing there crying. I was torn between eagerness to get away from him and fear of leaving him, but I finally pushed myself from the ground and made my way back to the safety of Mom.

In the most heart wrenching voice I have ever heard, she said, "John, please don't do this. Please don't leave us."

John, with tears rolling down his face, replied, "All I do is hurt everyone I love. I have stayed as long as I can. I am leaving you in good hands. Everyone would be better off if I was gone."

I was crying as hard as anyone else in the room. My voice was cracking from the tears, and I was gasping for breath as I pleaded, "Please don't leave me. I need you too much."

He turned his eyes toward the floor to avoid eye contact with us, but we could still hear him struggling to breathe and see his chest going in and out faster than normal. It was as if he were putting a boundary between us because it hurt him so much to see our faces.

Even intoxicated, John had thought through the entire morning. He knew Mom's first instinct would be to call for help. To squash that thought before she could act on it, he adamantly told her that she was not to call the police. If they were called, the ramifications would be dire. Of course, she told him that she wouldn't call them. What mother wouldn't lie to save her son? Either of us would have agreed to anything at that point if it meant saving him.

Granny Martha was one of the two exceptions that Mom was allowed to call. I'd like to think that John allowed her to be there for me and Mom, that he knew it was too much for us alone. Mom must have called her before I woke up, because Granny Martha appeared out of the fog. I turned to see her warm smile and feel her cold hand rest on my shoulder. I drew upon her strength and leaned in to allow her to carry the weight.

As she talked with John, her voice was soothing and calm, exactly what he needed. She spoke truth and faith in him as only she could have done. Her reassurance and plea gave him pause. Granny Martha accomplished something that Mom nor I could. He told her the only thing that would change his mind. John wanted to speak to his ex-girlfriend, Sara.

Giving us the first glimpse of hope, he said, "If Sara will come here and talk to me, I will not kill myself."

That was it, the way to change his mind, so we all raced down the stairs to the cordless phone in the living room to call her.

Mom spoke to Sara first, begging, "Please just come here and talk to him. He's really going to do it this time. I have never seen him this determined to do it."

Hearing those words, I thought, has he threatened this before? Why would he want to leave us? Why is he not happy with us? My mind snapped back into the present when I was handed the phone. I was crying so hard by this point that I only remember saying, "Please come help him."

Granny Martha took the phone from my ear and walked into the kitchen. I don't know what was said, but the answer was still no. She wasn't coming to help us. If we were going to save John, we would have to find another way.

Breaking her promise to John, Mom used the time away from him to call Chris, the chief of police of Neon, for help. The phone call came so early that he was still eating breakfast at Tootie's restaurant. I sat on the couch with a blanket wrapped around me as Mom paced through the dining room and explained the situation. "Chris, John is sitting in William's old bedroom with his back against the bed," Mom said. After a slight pause, Mom replied, "Yes, he has been drinking." Another pause. "No, I'm not sure how much," Mom replied. Chris had been to our home before, so he had a general idea of the layout. With what Mom had described and his memory of the home, he was able to give her an educated guess on how the interaction may play out.

Mom sat in one of the dining room chairs holding the phone without making a sound before pulling the receiver away from her ear and hitting the red button. She abruptly stood up and walked a few small steps to place the phone back on the charger base. After placing the phone on the charger, Mom relayed the conversation to Granny Martha in detail. Because of the way John was positioned in the first bedroom at the top of the stairs, he would hear the commotion on the steps. From the angle of the doorway and the hallway, he would see the police officers first and possibly shoot one or more. If they tried to enter through the window in the bedroom, John would see them in the antique vanity mirror on the wall. What the police chief was trying to prepare Mom for was the fact that if John shot at them, they would shoot back.

CHAPTER 14

The Sound

In less than 30 seconds, he went from talking to lifeless.

Chris was not permitted to respond to the complaint call by himself because of gun involvement. Following protocol, he requested backup from the Letcher County Sheriff Department. Because the request was made so early in the morning, it took longer for the deputy to arrive in Neon than it normally would have. It was assumed that we had more time than we did.

Chris and John had known each other for years. In fact, Chris had arrested him several times to keep him safe and then released him to Dad once he sobered up. John held no ill feelings toward Chris over the arrest. During a short stint, they worked together in the coal mines, when John gifted him a Harley-Davidson T-shirt. You must understand what a compliment that was. John loved anything Harley-Davidson and would have only given that type of a gift to someone whom he valued.

When I spoke to Chris before writing my book, he shared memories of the sober John, the one whom we all miss. Hearing someone else say, "John was always a hard worker and a man with a large heart when he was sober," was the sentiment I needed. I am grateful that others could see both sides of John. Chris's comments were a testament to what Dad had always preached to all of us, that you must always work, and work hard.

Mom was chain-smoking that morning. Every time I looked at her, she had a cigarette in her hand. Her eyes were glossed over from tears, but her love was so present. I could feel how much she loved John and how much she loved me. I could see in her shaking hands and stumbled-up words that she was trying so hard to be strong for me and him both. Her fight was slipping away, and defeat was seeping into her words as she continued to beg John not to take his life, as she asked for help from others. The only person holding Mom together was Granny Martha.

I can't imagine how Mom must have felt making the decision to allow or not allow the police to intervene. She did not want anyone else to get hurt. I believe she was still hopeful that we could change his mind. He had made threats before about suicide and not followed through. I can understand why she was holding on to that strand of hope. As the morning dragged on, John became more paranoid and angrier—he no longer allowed us to enter the bedroom. We could only stand in the doorway. I didn't understand at the time why he wouldn't allow us in the room any longer. Now as an adult, I assume it was one of two reasons: he feared we would try to take the gun or that our constant presence would sway his resolve.

John often became an angry drunk, and his ability to control his temper and actions were dismal at best. As the morning progressed, his temperament changed from resolute to devastated, and far more tears were flowing than words were spoken. We assumed the tears were of regret for the traumatic morning he had created, holding on to the hope that he was changing his mind. Just like the wind, the tears and regret would change to paranoia in an instant.

John was becoming more paranoid and irritated by any unusual or unnecessary moves. His attitude changed so abruptly and frequently that our heads were swiveling to keep up. Mom, Granny Martha, and I had been huddled around the doorframe for what seemed to be an eternity when Mom stepped back from the door and started walking toward the bedrooms at the end of the hallway. John's voice erupted, hollering, "Mom, what are you doing?"

I don't remember what Mom said, but I know that she lied. The real reason she was going down the hallway was to hide the other lose handgun in the house. There was a gun cabinet with some hunting guns, but she didn't have the key to it. Her hope was that if we could get the gun away from John, we had a chance of saving him. I believe he suspected that we might try to get the gun from him, which is why he kept us farther away from him. He was guarding the gun so closely—it was tucked under his leg with the end barely visible by this point of the morning. I don't know how we could have gotten ahold of it.

Mom was hopeful that the longer we delayed him from picking up the gun, the better our chances were of saving him. We were counting on the alcohol or lack thereof to change his mind. It was plausible that the longer we talked, the alcohol would start to leave his system. Therefore, as he started to sober up, he would change his mind about taking his own life. The other end of the spectrum was that the longer we talked, the more he would drink. We hoped that all the alcohol accompanied by no food would cause him to pass out. At the time both options seemed plausible but not probable. John had been drinking for so long that I am sure he knew his limits. The likelihood of him allowing himself to drink until he passed out that morning was slim.

We stood in the doorway talking to him until my legs ached. My body was overtaken by fatigue and hunger. I was exhausted from trying to make sense of the situation and just couldn't do it anymore. I sat down cross-legged on the floor in front of my mom and Granny Martha. I was eye level with John's chest, watching as it moved in and out while he cried. That morning our conversation was on repeat, pleading the same request over and over, pledging our love to him, and begging him not to leave us. It was as if we were unworthy and begging someone to stay with us.

Finally, it was midmorning, and our pleas had been heard. John looked at Mom with such sorrow and shame, saying, "I am so sorry, Mom. I can't believe I did this to you."

Mom cried, saying, "It's okay, John. I'm just glad you know that you were wrong."

I sat there on the floor with my mouth open slightly as I looked down at the floor, feeling relieved, as if a large weight had been taken off my shoulders. Finally, we could put this behind us.

In a somber tone, John asked, "Mom, would you mind fixing me some boiled eggs and coffee for breakfast?"

When I finally heard a request for breakfast, my eyes lit up. I was thinking, yes, please. Eating sounds like a great plan.

In a relieved tone, Mom said, "Of course," while turning to look at me. "Sissy, you stay here with John," she said.

She and Granny Martha disappeared down the stairs to fix the eggs and coffee, leaving John and me alone. That was the first time I had been alone with him since this nightmare started. I was scared and unsure of what to say or do and worried that I may cause him to change his mind.

As an adult I look back at that moment in time and realize that no child should fear her birth father or what he may do. I shouldn't have been put in a position to hold his life in my hands. I stood up in the doorway, leaning against one side, still crying while I said, "I love you, and I am so proud to be your daughter."

He looked at me with no emotions and said, "I love you too, Sissy."

He was sitting in his childhood home, broken with nowhere to turn. He had hit rock bottom and didn't have the energy to get back up. His tough-guy attitude and reputation were fading away. All that was left was a scared, helpless man who came home for peace. He looked smaller to me that morning, frailer than I ever thought possible. The cuss words and big actions were all a facade to hide his true feelings.

John said, "Go see if Mom has my food ready."

I resisted leaving, remembering that Mom told me not to leave him.

He looked at me with his green eyes and said, "Mom will need help carrying the food. Go help her."

I knew that if I hollered for Mom, it would be hard for her to hear me, because our kitchen was on the other side of the house. I hesitated to leave John, but I didn't think that he would lie to me, so I said okay. I turned and started walking down the stairs. As I stepped on the platform between the living room and my dad's CB room, I heard John holler, "I'm sorry, Sissy. I love you." Then the sound that changed everything rang through the house. It was loud and scary, as if a bomb had been detonated in our home. To me, the steps were vibrating. I don't know if that was from me being startled by the sound or from the gunshot itself.

Out of reflex, I ran back up the steps while a second loud sound rang through the house. I stopped at the doorframe that I was just standing in to see an image that changed me forever—the image of John lying life-less. Over the years that vivid image has faded and been confused with nightmares of the same incident. One image I see is his body still sitting cross-legged with the top part of his body hunched over his legs and his arms lying lifeless. The other image I see is his body lying on the floor with blood around his head and with his eyes open and looking at the door.

I believe the nightmares were a blessing. Because of the different im-ages in my mind, it's now easier for me to detach from them. I don't feel the intense emotions that I would have if I remembered perfectly how he looked.

My childhood was replaced by one shot. The life I knew was gone. I was standing surrounded by the shambles of what was once my family. In less than 30 seconds, he went from talking to lifeless.

It was all my fault, I thought—had I done what Mom told me to do, he would still have been alive. I chose to leave him alone, knowing there was a gun by his side. Allowing myself to trust him in that moment caused me to lose trust in others. I was a child, so why did he lie to me? Why did he put the guilt of his death on my shoulders? Not only had I let him down, but I also let down everyone else who loved him. In that moment I went from a child to an enabler. I transposed the anger I felt toward myself to how everyone else felt toward me.

It seemed like only moments later Mom and Granny Martha were standing behind me. Granny Martha shuffled Mom and me to her Cadillac that was parked at the top of the driveway. All three of us were cramped into the front seat with me in the middle. I could hear Mom heaving and feel her body shaking with distress and disbelief. She was crying uncontrollably while I sat numbly beside her. My young mind and heart had no idea how to process what just happened. My eyes had to be mistaken about what they saw. My ears had to be confused about the loud shaking sound that came through the house. My thoughts were snapped back to the present by the sight of the police car pulling into the driveway.

Chris and a Letcher County deputy sheriff had arrived to help us. We exited Granny Martha's car and walked down the driveway slowly, stopping on the concrete back porch for Mom and Granny Martha to explain the events that had transpired since the earlier phone call. The shock must have taken over my entire body because I don't remember being cold. I don't remember shivering from the cold. I was shaking from the shock of what I had just experienced. The police officers entered the house first, with us following behind them, almost as if we were afraid to enter in fear of what we may see or hear.

Standing in the sitting room and gazing into the kitchen, my mind trailed to my breakfast memories around the table, even though they were brief, I was longing for another cold morning around the table listening to John complain about another boring night at work while Mom rushed me to finish my breakfast and brush my teeth. How I wished I were at school with my friends rather than standing here.

Walking through the kitchen, Granny Martha suggested that I return to my bedroom, the bedroom where it all began that morning. By myself, I walked back to the room where I had lain asleep a few hours before all the madness occurred. I sat on the bed as Granny Martha, Mom, and the officers walked into the living room. I could hear Mom talking, but I couldn't make out what was being said. I felt as if I were eavesdropping on a private conversation as the grown-ups whispered. The whisper faded as the living room fell quiet. I sat on the bed listening for a hint of what was happening.

Chris and the other deputy started making their way up the steps slowly. Chris called out, "John, it's Chris. I just want to talk to you." No response. Chris repeated himself, "John, it's Chris. I just want to talk to you."

Again, there was no response. The officers turned the corner at the top of the stairs and saw John's lifeless body. Chris entered the room and verified that there was a heartbeat. He requested the Neon Ambulance Squad as he abruptly descended the stairs.

All four of the adults were standing in the living room talking when I heard the distant siren of the ambulance as it made its way up and around our hill. Our home was within town limits, only three to five minutes from the fire and police station, so the response time was extremely fast. We were also fortunate that Dad and William had volunteered for the fire department for years, so it was likely whoever was in the ambulance was someone we knew.

Looking out the bedroom window, I saw the bright swirling lights and heard the shrieking sound of the siren as the rescue squad passed our house to circle through the high school parking lot and slowly back into our driveway. Our driveway was rather steep and curved, so most people preferred to back in than back out.

The EMT and driver worked in unison as they opened the back doors of the ambulance, pulling the cot from inside and placing two duffle bags on it. They steered the cot down the driveway together. One of them must have held the door open as the other one navigated the cot through the back door and small sitting area. The sitting room was extremely small with room for only two chairs and a box television. The kitchen table and chairs had already been scooted over toward the windows so the cot could maneuver through the small area. Our once-safe haven was now overrun by strangers and unfamiliar noises.

Their presence was dominating Mom's attention and preventing me from being with her. Before they all arrived, I was able to see and hear her from the back bedroom. Now there was too much commotion for me to be able to see or hear her.

I kept feeling little flitters in my chest that increased every time someone walked through the dining room. My first thought was, Oh no, are they going to ask me questions? Will they blame me for what happened to

John? Could I be in trouble?

My mind raced until I felt nauseated. The sour taste in my mouth and the cold sweat that overtook my body made me lie over on the bed because I was too weak to hold myself up. I laid there, willing the sickness to pass so that I could get to Mom. Granny Martha tried to split her time between me and Mom, but Mom needed her more than I did. If asked, I would have told her to be with Mom, that I was okay.

Feeling slightly better, I rose from the bed, determined to see Mom. I slowly inched my way into the living room when I saw her talking to a man with a notepad in his hand. Later I figured out that he was one of the policemen asking questions about what occurred that morning. Standing in the doorway between the living room and the dining room, I listened as Mom answered questions about how events transpired that morning. Heartbroken, maybe in shock, she still found the strength to stand there and field questions that made her relive the worst event of her life. I didn't need a replay of the morning's events, I had experienced it all firsthand, so I went back to the bedroom. I just wanted to eat a bowl of cereal and watch TV. I wanted to do something normal for my age, something that didn't revolve around death or alcohol.

I was standing in the downstairs bathroom when I heard Mom shrill. It was a rattling-to-the-core, heartbreaking sound that caused me to dart out of the bathroom and into the bedroom. I was stopped in my tracks by seeing the cot wheeled past me. John's body lay lifeless with a white sheet covering him from his toes to his head.

I was only eight years old when I stood in my bedroom and watched his body being wheeled out of the house. I couldn't fully understand what his actions meant. I was concerned about his head being covered up. What if he couldn't breathe well under the sheet? What if the sheet covering scared him? I wanted him to be comfortable, not scared or struggling to breathe. I was relieved that he was finally being taken to the hospital. The doctors could fix anything, or so I thought.

CHAPTER 15
The Call

They still had a semblance of hope that John's body would recover and become self-sufficient.

The ambulance darted out of the driveway and around the hill before I made it to the window to steal one last glimpse of John. I was only steps from the bedroom window that looked onto the driveway, so for me to have missed even a glimpse of their exit, I must have been frozen in time.

Placing my hand on the cold window and stretching my neck to the left, I cried because he left his home alone. No one said goodbye. No one said, "I love you." Or did we? How could we not have uttered those words? Unable to support my body weight any longer, I gave into the weakness and allowed the window to be my crutch. My weight shifted onto the glass as I laid my forearm and forehead against the welcome coldness. Unaware of time or responsibility, I stood there wanting to be with John, to follow him to the hospital, and to crawl up in the bed with him and hug him until he felt better.

Instead, Mom and I stayed home that morning. We weren't in the waiting room as the doctors cut away John's clothes and placed IVs and machines to stabilize him. We didn't hold his hand while he waited for an ambulance to transport him to a trauma center. There was no one to pull the cover over his feet because he hated for his feet to be cold. Not together but each alone, we suffered—Mom in the living room with the police and visitors, me in the bedroom, and John at the hospital.

My legs wobbled like a toddler's as I made my way to the side of my bed. Falling onto the bed with a double bounce didn't provoke a giggle like usual. Instead, it just increased my nausea. A glancing look into the mirror resulted in a locked glare with someone I didn't recognize. My lips were turned down in a permanent frown, my eyes were hurting, and my face had red patches all over it.

The girl in the mirror was yelling back at me. "Because you made the wrong decision, everyone may lose John. You had one simple instruction to follow and that was to not leave him alone. How could you have been so stupid? Your family will not forgive you. You're going to be in big trouble over this. Your parents may not even keep you."

The familiar smell of cigarette smoke drifted through the house, which brought back the present and singular Brandi. The inner fighting ceased as I relaxed back on the bed and allowed my brain to calm. It was a familiar smell that meant one of my parents was close and that everything would be okay. Mom, Dad, and John had always smoked, so I grew accustomed to the smell, and in some ways, it was a soothing aroma.

I hoped that my body would be swallowed by the covers and provide an invisible shield between me and all the adults in the living room. The shield was my protector from questions and glaring eyes, and it served me well. For the most part, I was left to my own devices that morning. There was just an occasional peek in the door to make sure I was okay, or some semblance of okay. Lying there with only a small portion of my face showing, I drifted off to sleep.

Dad and William were at work, which left them both oblivious to the morning's events. Dad was deep in the side of a mountain digging coal when the mining operator radioed underground for him to come to the office immediately. Being hundreds of feet underground and working side by side with other men who all counted on each other made Dad's job tedious and demanding. With the length of the time it took him to get out of the mines, I'm sure his mind was running rampant with possible reasons why he was called out in the middle of a shift. Was he worried about his state trooper son or his alcoholic son? Did he worry that something was wrong with Mom or his mother-in-law? I wonder if the truth was worse than any of the possibilities that he imagined.

Dad called home after reaching the office to be informed by someone that his baby son had shot himself in his childhood home. I don't know who told Dad or how he handled the news. Was he comforted by his co-workers and boss, or did he even share the full story with them? Again, those are questions that I didn't ask and answers that he didn't divulge.

In his coal-covered clothes, Dad drove straight to the hospital to see his youngest son, the son whom he fought with and for over the years. Walking toward the emergency room doors, Dad saw the ambulance with its doors ajar, backed into the pit. Suspecting it was for John, he walked toward the ambulance.

As a volunteer at Neon Volunteer Fire Department Dad was familiar with sickness and even death. He was accustomed to transporting patients with family members following behind, hovering by the ambulance door. He wasn't familiar with being on the other side, being the family member instead of the driver. As he got closer, he saw his son lying on a gurney hooked up to machines that were designed to save his life.

Dad stole a brief minute with John before the ambulance doors were closed and the lights turned on. The ambulance pulled out of the bay in route to the trauma center in Lexington, Kentucky. Dad, standing alone and wiping his eyes with a dirty handkerchief, knew that he couldn't make the three-hour drive to be with his son. Out of either instinct or need, he came home to Mom and me.

My brother, William, was on duty with the Virginia State Police Department when he received the news of John's shooting. Dispatch radioed for him to call the office, and then he was told to call Ben, the sheriff of Letcher County. He returned Ben's call to learn that John had shot himself.

Three hours from home, William packed his bags and drove straight to our house. In that moment, he transitioned into the person in control with Mom and Dad doing as he said. They needed someone to take control of the situation, and he was the only person they trusted.

William was only a couple of years older than John, but William had served as his protector and enforcer for years. He was the follow-the-rules-and-do-what-was-right son. So, it made sense that he became a state trooper. My brother was always there for us even after he moved to Virginia. I was waiting for him to arrive home and fix everything. I knew that he would have all the answers.

The drive to Lexington was too daunting for both of my parents. Neither of them liked to travel, especially to a city they were unfamiliar with. Adding their uneasiness with travel to the pure shock and pain over John's shooting, they could not go. Seeing him confined to a bed with only machines keeping him alive was more than their shattered hearts could handle. Staying away from that mental image allowed hope to stay alive within their hearts.

Someone had to visit John and talk with the doctors in person, and that person was William. He was the only family member I know of who made the drive to Lexington to see John. He was the person who spoke with the doctors and who looked at his younger brother alive for the last time.

William shouldered the family responsibility of relaying information between our parents and the doctors. He didn't allow his pain to show. Instead, he stayed stoic for us. When he came home from seeing John, it was time for the family to make tough decisions, decisions that no one ever wanted to make. Telling our parents that John was indeed brain-dead had to be devastating. John's only claim to our world was bridged with breathing machines, IVs, monitors, and medicine.

Mom and Dad agreed to allow John to die naturally instead of being sustained by machines. Making that decision and believing it is truly the end are two different mindsets. They still had a semblance of hope that John's body would recover and become self-sufficient.

I don't remember the conversation that took place when Mom and Dad decided to remove John from the ventilator—maybe I was sent out of the room. Either way, I remember knowing that the next call from the hospital would tell us that John was dead. We expected the call to be soon since the machines were keeping him alive. Those minutes felt like an eternity as we waited for the doctor to call us.

The cordless phone was lying in front of William while he and I sat around the kitchen table. We sat in silence between the first and second call, the conversation to end John's life and the confirmation that he had passed away.

Both phones in the house had the ringers at the maximum volume since John's shooting, so it was easy to hear the phone ring no matter where you were in the house. It was so loud that it was startling if you were sitting near it. This phone call was different. I barely remember hearing it. I don't know if I was lost in my own thoughts or if William answered it before the first ring was finished. What I remember is the silence. There was no one speaking or moving except for William.

William answered the phone and stepped into the dining room to talk in private with the doctor. By the tone of the conversation, we knew it was the call we had dreaded. John had passed away. John's life came to an end when he was 29 years old. As William hung up the phone, I walked out of the kitchen into the dining room, crying, and said, "He's gone."

My brother bent down and scooped me up into his arms. As I cried with my head on his shoulder, he said, "I will always be here for you."

CHAPTER 16

The Start of Goodbye

At eight years old, I learned that you hurt more for
those you love than you hurt for yourself.

In a matter of seconds, the dining room morphed from a happy place into a cold, lonely room. The dark wood paneling walls were closing in around me as I stood still absorbing the news. The lights from the chandeliers flickered like candles in the wind. Dad's recliner was empty but still rocking, so he must have just stood up. The living room drapes and sheers were pulled tightly together to prevent the cold air from seeping in.

There was no visible sign of the outside world, just a rocking chair and dark wood paneling staring back at me. As I turned toward the kitchen, a faint glow from the overhead light provided a small walking path for me into the kitchen. The windows were covered with white lace curtains that allowed some outside light to peer through. The overhead light glowed dully, like an orange shade instead of a bright light. The dark cabinets and kitchen table didn't help to brighten up the room. The house had always been darker due to the colors and low-wattage bulbs, but it had never felt sad or dreary until then.

I was crying inside, crying for John and crying for the suddenness of my life turning upside down. My heart physically hurt, and my stomach felt constricted as if someone were sitting on top of me. My eyes were wet, but the tears didn't run down my face. Instead, I watched as my mom cried in a way that would bring a person to their knees. The pain across her face and the shaking of her body hurt me more than the news itself. Dad cried but not like Mom—he buried his pain deep inside and stayed stoic for us.

Within a few hours after John passed away, our house was filling up with family and friends. Our door was a revolving entryway, which provided a reprieve if only for a minute. The consistent company kept some of the loneliness at bay. Focusing on conversations and an occasional laugh allowed us to escape reality. Family members and friends flocked to Mom to try and comfort her, but how do you comfort someone from such a tragic loss? There were no words that could provide healing or peace during those hours.

Our community's love language was food. We provided for one another in time of need. Mom couldn't cook after John's shooting, and William was already handling so much. That's where our family and friends stepped in. They carried in casseroles, cakes, sandwiches, snack food, and drinks until our refrigerator and cabinets were overflowing. Food has always served as a comfort for me. I tend to eat during stressful and sad times. Having snack food so readily available made it easy for me to grab a snack and go to the bedroom or to the living room without being an inconvenience.

During that week Mom didn't limit my sugar intake. I was free to drink as much pop and eat as many sweets as I could handle. I took full advantage of that opportunity by eating my sadness away. I would have candy bars or individual snack cakes hidden with my Barbie dolls so that I didn't always have to go into the kitchen where the adults were talking.

Walking into the kitchen was emotionally draining. That was Mom's place to grieve and talk with her family and friends. She would sit at the kitchen table with her ashtray, chain-smoking with a trembling hand, her eyes red and puffy. She forced a small smile when she saw me, but I saw the pain behind the smile.

During those days, my home didn't feel like my own. I didn't have a place that I could just go and be—I was always in someone's way. The grown-ups were trying to shield me from the sadness by asking me to leave the room. What they didn't realize was I lived it every day, every minute.

I still heard the tears and saw the pain. There was no shielding me from that sadness.

I would rotate between the kitchen, living room, and my back bedroom depending on who was visiting and what the conversation was regarding. The only room I wasn't asked to leave was my bedroom. Lying in the bed, I could still hear the conversation in the kitchen. There was no sound blockade or background noise to distract me. Sometimes I listened to their conversations; other times I allowed myself to daydream about a different life for me and my family, one of joy and happiness.

During one of those lonely days, my older cousin Sandra, Mom's niece, spent time with me. Instead of talking with the adults, she and I lay across the bed talking. I don't remember much of what we talked about—I was just grateful she was there with me. Having a small amount of one-on-one attention helped more than the grown-ups realized.

I have a memory of a preacher from a local church coming to our house to talk with Mom and Dad. Sitting on the edge of the couch and holding his Bible, he bowed his head and prayed for comfort and peace for our family. He asked God to hold us in his hands as we dealt with the tragedy we were facing. After the prayer, he shared a few Bible verses with us about God's love and how he could help us. The preacher made a plea for our family to attend church and look to God for healing. Mom and Dad believed in God but didn't go to church. So, his plea was not received.

I have a memory of him saying the cruelest thing a person could say to our family: "Committing suicide is a sin. Your son went to hell if he didn't repent." That wasn't the message we needed to hear at that moment. We had so many questions, so much pain, and so much anger that our world was unrecognizable. Adding more worry about John was too much to carry.

I wasn't a little girl who got dressed up often or curled my hair. I was more of a casual-play-clothes type of kid with tangles in my hair. So, putting on a frilly dress, tights, and dress shoes wasn't something I enjoyed. I did it reluctantly when I had to. When it was time to get dressed for night one of John's viewings, I wasn't happy with the clothes that someone had laid out for me. I walked into the downstairs bedroom, and there were tights and a dress lying across the bed with a pair of black patent leather shoes sitting on the floor. I put on the dress without much fuss because there was too much sadness and anger already swirling around our house.

The reasoning behind wearing our Sunday best to a funeral escaped me. I had no desire to put on a pretty dress with tights or patent leather shoes. That outfit was reserved for special moments, moments when I wanted to look beautiful as I swirled around in my dress, not on evenings when I was sad and didn't feel like smiling.

My first experience with death and funerals occurred the previous summer. My paternal grandmother passed away. Prior to Grandma being transferred to a nursing home near Pikeville, we would visit with her, my aunt, uncle, and cousins occasionally. Once she entered the nursing home, I only went a few times with Dad to visit. Grandma had struggled with diabetes for years and no longer felt up to visitors, especially young kids. The last time I remember seeing her, I cried because of how frail and disengaged she was. She no longer got out of bed and rarely sat up when visitors came. Instead, her only movement was when the nurses rotated her body. I walked over to show her my toy, but she barely had the energy to acknowledge me. The lack of interaction and inability to talk frightened me, so Dad didn't take me back after that visit.

Dad wasn't a man who showed a lot of emotion, so to see him cry was rare. I witnessed the sadness and crying of family members at Grandma's funeral, but I didn't grasp the significant impact that death had on the living. It was hard for me to comprehend that someone would leave this earth and that I would not see them again till heaven. It seemed to give the adults comfort, this magical place called heaven, so again, I accepted it as something I would understand later.

I felt a little more prepared for the logistics of John's funeral since I had attended Grandma's the previous summer. Family and friends would mingle with one another, talking, laughing, and crying. Hugs would be exchanged, and sympathies would be expressed over the three days. In our hometown most viewings were held for two evenings with the funeral and graveyard procession on the third day. Some families chose to have a short service consisting of singing and prayer during the nightly viewing, while others only used that time to spend with family or friends. It was based on individual preference.

I feared John's funeral would be different for me. The pain was more prominent, and the loss felt more real than when Grandma Isaac had passed away five months earlier. There would be no more meals around the kitchen table or sitting on the front porch together, no more ice cream outings or pretend fishing trips in a mud puddle above the house. I had not yet fully processed how different my life would be without him and how the house and our family would never be the same again.

At eight years old, I learned that you hurt more for those you love than you hurt for yourself. I worried about my mom and dad. I worried about how they would be able to say goodbye to him. I wondered if Mom would collapse like my aunt did at Grandma's funeral. My stomach was in knots trying to determine what was and was not appropriate for me to say or do at the funeral home. Mom and Dad had so much to worry about. I didn't want them to worry about me too. More than anything I wanted their pain to stop. I wanted them to be happy again.

As we pulled into the parking lot of the funeral home, I was intimidated by the number of guests who had gathered to support our family. The large covered front porch was full of family and friends overflowing into the yard. Most of the faces were running together. I didn't know who most of the people were, so I kept my head down. No eye contact meant not speaking.

Mom and Dad made their way through the crowd as people hugged them, touched their arms, or nodded at them. Several people spoke to me, but most of them gave me a sad smile, where their lips were closed, and their mouths went straight out instead of upward.

The funeral director greeted us at the front door with yet another sad smile. "No one has been in to see John. I was waiting for you to see him first."

"That doesn't matter," Dad said. "You could have let them in."

Mom didn't respond or acknowledge what either of them said. My parents decided to disregard the immediate-family visitation and allowed everyone to enter the funeral home with us.

I wonder if allowing others to enter the funeral home at the same time was easier for them. Instead of taking the time to pay their respects to John, they were able to focus on the guests. With so many people floating through the funeral home, they didn't have to fully accept that their son was lying in the front of the room. In a sense the guests served as a distraction from the pain and reason we were all gathered that evening.

The small funeral home foyer served as a roadblock of sorts—everyone had to stop in that room to sign John's guestbook and pick up an obituary. The room was not inviting or colorful. Instead, it featured wood paneling and muted wallpaper with two oversized floral chairs that swallowed you as you sat in them. I couldn't imagine sitting in that room for any length of time. In winter it would be too cold with the door opening and closing, and in the summer, it would be too hot for the same reason. From the foyer we entered the chapel that held John's casket. His lavender casket was placed prominently in the front of the chapel with the top lid ajar. From the side of the room, you could see the top of his head resting on a white silk pillow. Leaning on the lid was a single rose for each of his three children: me and my two half sisters. Draped over the bottom of the casket lid was a gorgeous floral spray.

John had on a pastel multicolor button-up shirt with a lavender sweater over it. Fearing the worst for John, William packed the sweater and shirt for him to wear if needed. John wasn't the type to dress up. He wore Harley-Davidson T-shirts, boots, and jeans, so seeing him in a sweater was a shock to me. He didn't look like himself lying there. It wasn't the way he wore his hair—they had it fixed perfectly, whereas he had kept his wavy brown hair free flowing. His face was covered with a thick foundation. His hands were freezing and stiff. It was as if someone else were lying in the casket. I wondered how he could look so different in just a few days.

Seeing John's body in the casket didn't affect me in the way one might think it would have. It didn't look like him. He looked like a life-size human doll inside of a pretty box. The makeup applied to his face, neck, and hands was thick and orange tinted. His arms lay crossed over his abdomen, stiff and hard like a doll in a package. Had he looked more like himself, it may have been harder to say goodbye.

Mom couldn't bring herself to enter the visitation room in fear of catching a glimpse of John. The thought of seeing her youngest son lying in a casket was more than she could bear. She and I already had a haunting image burned into our memories from the day of John's shooting. So, she chose to stay in the funeral home's kitchen area.

The compact kitchen was composed of a small round wooden table and four straight-back chairs strategically placed in the center of the room. A single kitchen counter ran along one side of the wall where a hot coffee machine, stacks of white Styrofoam cups, and powdered mixes were laid out. The freshly brewed coffee aroma wafted out into the hallway and entryway of the funeral home providing a trail for guests to follow.

It was as if the adults were drawn to the coffee. So many of them walked around holding a white Styrofoam cup with steam bounding out the top, I don't know how there weren't more spills and people burned. The only drink for noncoffee drinkers was an RC pop machine that was strategically placed along the wall that connected the kitchen to the back door. The peach Nehi were the best in my opinion. I cannot even start to recall how many of them I drank during the viewing.

The kitchen was intended to provide a reprieve from the heavy heartache felt in the visitation room and to serve as a place to regroup and regain composure as needed. For Mom, it wasn't a reprieve. Instead, it was a hideaway from realization. That small room protected her from the acceptance of losing her son.

Daddy split his time between the viewing room and the front porch.

The front porch was where the visitors gathered to smoke and talk—yet another place you could escape from the heartache of the visitation room. Dad's friends and coworkers seemed to keep him preoccupied during most of the viewing.

I knew our days with John were numbered, and every second was ticking closer to our final goodbye. There would be no more touching his cold, hard hands or looking at his thick hair brushed back from his face. There would be no more face-to-face conversations, even if they were one-sided, silent conversations. Standing by his casket, I had internal conversations that only he and I could hear. I felt compelled to be near him to soak in every moment that we had together before I had to say goodbye.

CHAPTER 17
The Last Time

*At eight years old, I had simplistic feelings—I missed
John and wanted him to still be with us.*

The funeral home was full of familiar faces during the viewing. For some, I could recall their names—others, only their faces. Both of my parents had rather large extended families that came together to support one another during the difficult times. So many people approached me, introducing themselves and giving me side hugs, that I could hardly keep count. I tried to smile and be friendly, but it was difficult. Adults were trying so hard to comfort me, but what can you really say to a young girl who is oblivious to death and God?

"Brandi, John is in heaven now. He is no longer suffering."

I wanted to ask how he was suffering here with us. Why was he better in heaven? But I knew better than to ask those questions, so I nodded and smiled.

"John's body is no more than an empty vessel. His soul is in heaven."

"Empty vessel" or "empty body" was hard to hear. That was him lying in the casket, all of him, so how could part of him just be gone?

"He will always be with you. You can talk with him anytime."

I liked the premise of that statement but didn't understand how it could be true if he was indeed gone.

I believe each person had the best intentions at heart. They were searching for words or phrases that would help me understand the finality of John's death. I just wasn't ready to hear them or old enough to compre-hend the coined phrases. There were no words that could provide comfort or understanding during those days. At eight years old, I had simplistic feelings—I missed John and wanted him to still be with us.

No one missed John more than Mom. Her eyes were hollow, with no shine or life in them. Her voice sounded raspy and winded, and her laugh was nonexistent. More than anything, I missed my mom and wanted her to be okay. I understood why John always turned to her because I did the same thing. Seeing the most important person in your world heartbroken hurt worse than any pain I felt for myself.

For the better part of the evening, I roamed around the funeral home left to my own devices. Whenever I was given the opportunity on my rounds through the funeral home, I hovered close to Mom, but she was usually surrounded by family and friends. Being close to Mom made every-thing better—the fear, the sadness, and the anger.

During the first night of the viewing, Lynn, William's girlfriend, and I went to Mike Johnson's Drive-In for dinner. I wasn't very hungry but would never turn down one of their famous chili buns and cheese sticks. Mike's was located on the other end of town, so maybe five minutes away from the funeral home. I climbed into the front seat of Lynn's Bronco like a big girl and wrapped the seat belt around me just as William always said we had to do. A little uncomfortable and unsure of what to say, I waited for Lynn to lead the conversation.

"So, what's your favorite food at Mike's?" Lynn asked.

"Chili bun with cheese sticks," I replied sheepishly. Part of me was uncomfortable with Lynn, not because of anything that she did. I felt as if I wasn't good enough to be with her. She was always well dressed, her hair and makeup perfectly fixed, while I usually looked disheveled, walking around with tangles in my hair or with it brushed but just hanging down my back. Mismatched or play clothes adorned my body. How could I ever fit in with her?

We pulled into Mike's parking lot and walked up to the window to place our order. She let me tell the lady what I wanted to eat.

"A chili bun, cheese sticks, and vanilla milkshake, please," I said, like a big girl.

After paying for our order, we went back to her Bronco to wait for the lady to wave us back to the window. Shivering from the cold, she turned the heat up to high as she asked, "So how is school?"

"I love it," I replied. "Mrs. Vanover is the best teacher. We have playtime every day, even when it's cold outside. The merry-go-round is my favorite part of recess, even though I feel sick after riding it. Heather and some of my other friends play basketball, but that's not as much fun for me. I would rather climb the monkey bars and watch everyone from above."

Lynn just listened as I rambled on about my friends and favorite activities at school. I was playing nervously with a small tear in my tights. She noticed and said, "You have a run in your tights." A little embarrassed, I looked at her as she pointed to the small fray above my leg. "I can fix it for you," she said, as she pulled her purse from the back seat. Pulling out clear fingernail polish and gently brushing it over the fray, Lynn smiled and said, "This will keep it from running further." It worked. The small tear didn't spread any further. Rubbing my fingers over the tear, I could tell the difference—it was sticky and thick but unnoticeable to the naked eye.

Walking back into the funeral home, I was greeted with the same sadness and anger that was swirling before we left. Family and friends were floating from one clique to another, some crying, while others were talking. Mom was staying distant from most people, only confiding in her small circle. Dad was buzzing around talking to everyone. He really was a social butterfly and knew practically everyone there. Making my way through the crowded funeral home, I claimed a front-row seat in the viewing room. While I sat there alone quietly, my insides were screaming for John to wake up and look at me. I so wanted him to tell me that it was just a bad joke, that he was here and alive, that I would never lose him again.

It seemed as if the viewing had both lasted hours and only a few minutes. I was emotionally and physically exhausted from the day and craved rest but felt guilty for wanting to leave the funeral home. It was difficult walking out of the funeral home and leaving his body there alone. I felt that we were abandoning him, but I had no one I could share those feelings with. So, instead I sat in the back seat of the car and allowed the tears to roll down my face quietly.

The morning of the funeral, everyone except for Mom and Aunt Donna gathered into the visitation room. Mom was completely against seeing John in the casket or participating in the funeral proceedings. For her, it was too real to see his body lying there without life. I don't think she had the strength to endure saying goodbye, so she chose to hide. Aunt Donna opted to stay with Mom, because no mother should be alone during such a horrifically painful time.

All the floral arrangements stationed around the front and side of the dreary chapel added much-needed color to the room. Some were cut flowers, and others were silk arrangements, each beautiful. Some of the attached cards were difficult for me to read, but I did recognize the one sent from my homeroom teacher and class. The card attached read, "Love, Mrs. Vanover's Homeroom class." That simple flower arrangement meant I had some form of normalcy that I could return to when ready. Those flowers made me feel still included and missed.

The day of the funeral, I don't remember who I sat beside or what songs were sung. I only remember feeling alone and helpless. My dad was crying, my mom was devastated, and I was so confused. I wanted to make it better for everyone, but I didn't know what to do. As a safety mechanism, my body shut down during the service. I sat there in a daze that blocked out all sounds and vision. For me, it's almost as if the service didn't happen. I was in a different realm, like Mom was, only my body was there in the present.

The shiny black hearse led John's extensive funeral procession from the funeral home in Neon to the family graveyard in McRoberts. Lined up bumper-to-bumper, we took our last ride together, all of us with John, past my school and home. The road was so familiar that most of our family could have driven it blindfolded and not missed a turn. The short 10-minute ride wasn't long enough for us to be prepared to say goodbye. The country road was practically empty that morning. The few cars that we saw pulled onto the curb of the road to pay their respects. The trees had lost all their leaves, so the mountains looked dead and dreary. The old coal camp houses alongside the road were bland with most of the greenery dead for the season. It was a sad, somber ride that wasn't easy to be present for.

The small one-lane hollow that led us to Grandma's farm was narrow, so narrow that there were very few places that two cars could pass. Accommodating a large funeral procession or parking multiple cars in such a tight area wasn't easy. It took the funeral directors and several family members awhile to help get everyone to a safe place. Even then, some ended up being parked on the edge of the road.

McRoberts was home for most Mom's side of the family, including Grandma Sparks. It was a second home to almost everyone else in the family. A place that you could return to your roots and find peace when life was crazy. Grandma Sparks was a grounding force for all her kids and grandkids. Her home was a place that you were safe and loved.

It was fitting that a portion of the farm that was no longer being utilized was turned into a family graveyard. A piece of land that had raised most of the family would now provide a final resting place and solitude for those who had passed on. It was a beautiful sentiment and exactly what our family needed at that moment. John grew up loving Grandma and the farm. He often told Grandma that he wanted to be buried on the hill behind the barn. Grandma always placated John without giving it much thought. The thought of him passing away before her wasn't even a possibility in her eyes.

When the worst happened and Mom needed a place to bury her son, William stepped in and asked Grandma if John could be buried on the hill behind the barn. Of course, Grandma obliged, and that started the Sparks family cemetery.

The pallbearers hoisted the heavy coffin from the back of the hearse and started making the trek up the steep hill. Due to the length and steepness of the hill, we had people stepping in and out carrying the casket; it was too much for just a few men. Mom and Dad were directly behind John as we started up the hill. I was a little farther back, walking with my cousins Sandra and Tammy. Prior to reaching the barn, Mom started asking where I was. She wanted me with her. I don't know if it was to give me support or so I could give her support. Either way, we walked hand in hand up the hill behind John, crying.

CHAPTER 18
Lonely Days

I was carrying a heavy weight that others didn't see or know about,
because I feared my sadness would be too much for Mom to bear.

Healing from losing a loved one, whether it's expected or sudden, hurts you to your core. I felt extreme pressure sitting on top of my chest, the type that makes you struggle to breathe. My eyes that once glowed back at me in the mirror were hazed over by tears and puffy from lack of sleep. The deep frown and distant stare resembled someone who was no longer inside her body. Life circled around me like a tornado transporting me from an innocent child to an adult world.

The morning after John's funeral, I lay motionless, curled into the fetal position with the covers tightly cocooning me and allowing only my face to be seen in the dresser mirror against the wall. The blurry reflection glaring back at me in the mirror was of a young girl who lacked the energy to rise from her warm bed. I lay there listening intently for familiar sounds that would provide a sense of normalcy. Instead, I only heard the coal furnace blowing air through the floor vents. There was no talking or muffled TV in the distance.

The aroma of coffee seeping through the house ensured that both parents were awake, and considering that the coffee pot was not percolating, they must have been up for at least a short time. I wondered why Mom wasn't listening to the morning news or a talk show, or why Dad wasn't listening to his CB radio and scanner. Why were they so quiet? Did they not want to wake me? That had never been a concern before. It was baffling to me that they were both sitting on opposite sides of the house not talking to anyone or following what was once their normal routine.

We all made our way around the house like zombies, not following our normal routine or interacting with each other. It was an eerily quiet time in our house between the funeral and when I returned to school.

Being back in school with a semi-normal routine was helpful for me. It offered a reprieve from the sadness and memories that were consuming our home. Being free to play and act like a kid instead of worrying about being too loud or having too much fun was a relief. It was also helpful that my third-grade teacher was the mother of my best friend, Heather. Heather and I had been practically inseparable since kindergarten. The friendship that Heather and I built is what carried me through those early years of school. I knew that I always had a friend who would be there with me.

Heather's friendship was the one constant before and after John's death. Her mom still allowed her to come home with me after school regularly to play, without a second thought. When we were old enough for sleepovers, Heather was allowed to stay at our house anytime. To her family, it was as if the incident with John didn't happen. They helped me adjust back to school after John's suicide by being supportive and encouraging. They didn't allow others' opinions of me or my family to change how they saw me.

Unfortunately not everyone was as kind. A few days after returning to school, I experienced my first emotional attack in the girls' bathroom. I walked into the downstairs bathroom to hear chattering and laughing. I could tell by the voices that it was a few of the popular girls who were only nice when they needed something but ignored me when I wasn't useful. Keeping my distance, I went in the stall farthest away from them. Using the bathroom, I listened as one of the girls said, "Mom told me that I am not allowed to go to Brandi's anymore because of what her dad did."

Another girl responded, "Yeah, I can't believe he shot himself."

"Mom said he was drunk, as usual."

Standing only a few stalls over, I wished I could have melted into the drain and floated away. My face flushed from anger, and tears burned my eyes as they rolled down my cheeks. I stood there frozen until they left the bathroom, not wanting them to see my tears or the pain across my face. I was not going to give them the satisfaction of knowing they had hurt me.

I was so young and naive at the time of John's death that I didn't realize that committing suicide was such a heinous sin. I didn't know there were tiers of "acceptable" ways for someone to die. Furthermore, I had no idea that friendship was based on the tier on which a loved one passed away. It didn't take long for the kids more well versed in the world to make me aware that John had committed an ultimate sin. Some of them smirked at me as the words "You're weird," or "Your family is crazy," rolled off their tongues. Worse yet, one of them said, "Oh gross, I'm not sitting beside you," as if suicide were contagious! What?!?

To fortify myself from further heartache and pain, I started to construct walls around my heart. I knew then that I couldn't allow others the satisfaction of knowing they had hurt me, even though they did hurt me, even though I held on to every comment that was made. My outside persona didn't show it.

Yes, those general statements did hold truth, but it wasn't the entire truth. You cannot paint an individual as all bad or all good; they are indeed a mixture of both. Those kids thrived on making backhanded comments about John's suicide and my birth family. Since I came from such a "bad family," they were not allowed to play at my house.

I was grateful that I only had a few weeks of school before Christmas break. Even though I loved the escape from the sadness, I also felt embarrassed and self-conscious around the other kids. It seemed as if I was no longer completely comfortable anywhere. The rest of the kids were buzzing with excitement about the upcoming Christmas holiday. Fellow classmates were speculating about what gifts they would receive or the family they would see over the holiday break.

With only three weeks between John's death and our first Christmas without him, the excitement was minimal. So much of that time is a blur to me, with only brief flickers of memories that evoke joy and tears. That Christmas season taught me two important life lessons. First, it is so important to take care of those in need. Second, family can change after a death.

Our Christmas tree that had always been hoisted up from the basement was once again in its rightful place, in front of the living room picture window. Tinsel and garland were wrapped loosely around the tree branches with flickering lights glowing through the decorations. The tree skirt was secured around the metal stand with presents lying underneath.

Christmases past, you could feel the holiday spirit and excitement throughout the entire house. The oversized Christmas tree was adorned with red and green bubble lights that flickered through the silver tinsel and garland. Homemade ornaments hung lumped together on branches close to the bottom, and an angel shone brightly from the top of the tree. The sheer number of presents seemed to double every few days until Christmas Eve. Usually by then I had a stack of presents taller than I was.

The coffee table in the front of the living room displayed a Santa with his sleigh full of presents centered on a lace doily. Collectible Christmas homes and candles filled the top of the wooden box TV. The Christmas lights hung on the front porch shone brightly through the front living room window.

The dining room table was decorated with a deep-red table linen and gold placemats at each seat. Above the table a red bell with a small piece of holly hung from the chandelier. The bell played a short melody as people walked past—the motion sensor was often turned off by one of the adults. Atop the buffet, a coordinating scarf lay draped over with a floral arrangement in the center and a tall pillar candle on each side.

The kitchen was where the magic happened. The table and counters were covered with homemade desserts, fruits, and nuts. Mom would work for days making homemade peanut butter fudge, chocolate–peanut butter combo fudge, chocolate fudge, cream puffs, and chocolate pie, among other things. There was always a special dessert readily available. Dad would often sneak into the kitchen and grab handfuls at a time as if Mom would have scolded him, which she wouldn't have. It was cute to watch them interact over the sweets, bantering back and forth. For those non-sweet lovers, if there is such a person, a wooden nut bowl was always filled to the brim with holiday mixed nuts. Perched in the center of the bowl was a singular silver nutcracker and little silver picks to pry the nut open with.

The entire house smelled like cinnamon potpourri from small containers placed on the heat vents in every room downstairs. That was the scent of Christmas during my childhood. I always thought the bags of mixed potpourri were pretty, but I learned quickly not to pick them up because the scent would transfer to my hands. Once that scent was on my hands, it took a lot of scrubbing and soap to wash it off.

Our Christmas feast took several days to prepare. Starting two days prior to dinner, Mom would pull out her large cast iron skillet and bake two pones of cornbread, followed by baking two rolls of the small country biscuits. Once all the baking was completed, she would place them in a large covered silver cooker for them to sit overnight.

The next day she would shred the cornbread, biscuits, and light bread into a big silver bowl and mix it together without squeezing, because overworking it would make it tough. Then she would add salt, pepper, and sage. Sage was what made the dressing taste good. If you didn't add enough, it was bland; if you put too much, it was bitter. The person mixing the dressing together couldn't trust their own sense of smell when it came to the sage, so someone else always had to perform the sniff test. If Dad was home, he would do it; if not, one of us would fill in for him. The final steps required onions, celery, eggs, butter, and a little cream. Once the dressing was mixed well, we patted it out into small patties for baking. Oh, how I loved Mom's dressing. It wasn't a family holiday meal without it.

The shucky beans were green beans that had been strung on twine and hung in the sun to dry. Once the beans were wilted, brown, and brittle, they were unstrung, broken into small pieces, and frozen. To reach the thickness and flavor desired, the beans needed two full days of cooking. Dad would hover around the kitchen close to dinnertime on day one, hoping that Mom would let him have a small bowl to taste test, which she usually did. Sitting at the kitchen table with a big bowl of beans, a sliced onion, and cornbread, he would rave about how good it tasted. I hated the brown beans but always ate a small bite every holiday because they were part of our family tradition. Still today, I will eat a small spoonful just to keep the memory alive.

The day of the dinner, Mom would spend hours preparing the rest of the food, such as ham, potato salad, and vinegar deviled eggs. When she was finished, the cabinets were covered with food options—truly too much for one family to eat, which always meant leftovers. I would eat those leftovers until they were gone or Mom would toss them out.

Prior to opening gifts, everyone had to finish eating. For adults with bigger mouths than ours, it sure did take them a long time to finish their dinners. My cousin Nicole and I were often finished before they had barely started. Of course, we nagged and begged them to hurry, which probably slowed them down more than sped them up. Finally, after everyone was finished, William would divide out the presents in stacks for each of us. Sometimes Nicole and I opened presents together; other times we went from youngest to oldest, which meant I was the last kid to open my presents.

The Christmas after losing John didn't hold the same magic or joy. We were all still reeling from the pain and confusion that we had just faced a few weeks before. I am sure Mom and Dad felt compelled to give me the Christmas I was used to, but grieving was overtaking their lives too.

Others in our community understood their position and stepped in to help without being asked. Our family and friends hadn't forgotten us after John's death. Instead, they supported us during the Christmas season. The stack of presents from friends and family was growing infinitely taller than the tree. My curiosity and excitement got me in trouble a few times because I tried to peek into the pretty, wrapped presents.

I cannot even begin to give credit to all of those who rang our doorbell during the holiday season, because the outpour was too great. So many people carried in gifts, food, candies, and pies that our house was overflowing with Christmas love. Their simple acts of kindness far exceeded the gifts themselves—the lasting gift was the feeling they left our family with.

Throughout the years I still think of that holiday season and realize how fortunate we were to have people in our lives who showed us what true love was. The reason we made it through that first holiday season was because of the support and outreach from others. I am so eternally grateful for our community and the love they showed when we needed it the most.

Those early years after John passed away, there were a lot of lonely days for me, Mom, and Dad, especially during the holidays. Starting on Christmas Eve, I would pace from the living room window to the kitchen window, watching for company. We had family come in and out, but they couldn't stay long due to other family obligations. It was so hard to watch others pour into the house, sharing stories of where they had been and whose house they were going to next while we sat there alone.

CHAPTER 19

Lasting Effects

*They were both fulfilling their previous duties
but with a little less momentum.*

Depression wasn't only taking over my life; it was consuming Mom as well. Her routine was the same, but her energy and enthusiasm were depleted. Her footsteps no longer echoed through the dining room on her way to the kitchen. "Brandi Dawn" was no longer said with a booming voice. Mom's thick glasses couldn't hide the emptiness and pain in her eyes. Her response time to a question was delayed. Reflexes were slower and less animated. Mom's monotone voice and slumped appearance were hard not to notice.

I wonder if others saw the sadness in my eyes or if I did a decent job of hiding it. Were others concerned that I was depressed? Or did they believe I was too young to suffer from depression? Back then, when things were sad and lonely, Mom and I formed a bond—a unified bond over our mutual reality of depression and anger. Even though neither of us openly acknowledged those feelings, we found a kindred spirit within one another.

I felt at peace with her, as if I could fully be myself—flaws and all—without worry of judgment. I knew that she understood the trauma that I had experienced and that she didn't judge me or push me when I made decisions that were less than stellar. We protected each other even when the other was wrong. We stood together.

Mom's small sitting room was once a joyous place where she focused on her hobbies, whether it was sewing, crocheting, or reading. She often had a paperback book lying on the table with a small piece of paper serving as a bookmark, or she had a square from a quilt that she was working on lying on a shelf. The room was a representation of her and always a happy place to be.

After John passed away, the lights were not turned on as often. The books became fewer and further between. She would sit there, facing the wall with a far-off stare. Her profile view from the kitchen showed only movements to take a draw of her cigarette. Sometimes the tip of the cigarette was the only light in the room, which used to be lit by the TV or her small lamp. On her side table would either be a brown coffee mug or a blue-and-red Pepsi can.

At night, after Mom thought I was asleep, I would hear the phone receiver click and Mom clear her throat. I knew she was either calling Granny Martha, Aunt Donna, or Grandma. Those were the only three people whom she openly talked to about John.

Crying, she always asked, "How do I go on? I should have done more to help him. Now he is gone, and I am still here." She blamed herself for not protecting John. Whoever was on the other line was not able to give Mom the advice she needed because the calls continued for months.

It seemed as if Mom's face aged overnight after John's death. Her once-vibrant face was now lifeless and drooping like someone recovering from a stroke. The puffiness and dark circles under her eyes shone through her thick bifocal glasses. Her thick, wavy hair was becoming thin and brittle. Simultaneously she was falling apart both emotionally and physically due to the pain consuming her heart. The mom who I knew for the first eight years of my life withered away to someone who was only a shell of herself.

Emotionally there was a detachment and anger that changed Mom's soul. Things that she once enjoyed became more of a chore for her, such as cooking, decorating our home for Christmas, or playing with me. My heart broke for my mom because I saw the devastation and heartbreak in her face and heard it in her voice. My only desire was for her to be okay.

I always remembered Dad stretched out in his oversized tan recliner in his CB room, a.k.a. his man's den. The room was barely bigger than a closet, but he didn't complain. Instead, placed to the right of his chair, he had a small rickety table that held his scanner, and on the left, a set of homemade shelves held several CB radios and parts to miscellaneous items. With the scanner inches from his ears, it was still cranked up to the loudest volume possible. I could easily hear it in my bedroom. Before John died, Dad would jump up and repeat everything he heard on the scanner, like a little gossiper, but after John's death, Dad didn't even listen to the scanner. Instead, it was background noise as he stared into the unknown.

Dad went back to work and worked harder and longer than before, because he needed a way to channel his grief. For him, work was an outlet that allowed him the ability to block out his thoughts and pain. Being home and sitting idle gave his mind and heart time to process what had occurred under his roof. I am sure on some level he blamed himself over John's death, I guess we all did, but he never openly said that to me. Dad wasn't the type to discuss his feelings—instead he either buried them or resolved them within himself. Either way, he rarely told me how he felt unless I asked. Still, it wasn't the full truth—it was always, "Well, baby, Daddy's okay."

They both were trying to figure out how to live without their son and raise a daughter who was originally their granddaughter. The strength that it took for them to pull it together for me is unmatched by anything I have seen. I can't imagine how hard it was to get up and take care of a small child every day without a break. But they did it. They did it for me. After experiencing so much loss myself, I understand the effort it took for them to push through each day, to make sure dinner was on the table, to get up for work every morning, and to attend my extracurricular activities.

I could tell they were only going through the motions—there was no enjoyment or urgency in anything they did. Mom's lack of energy was evident by the way she walked slower with smaller steps and the fact that she sighed when sitting and rising from a chair. Even though they were drained, my parents still tried their best to give me a normal life. I would like to think that my presence helped them to regain a semblance of the life they had. Knowing that I needed them kept them putting one foot in front of the other.

Slowly, they started to readjust back to the way they were before John's suicide, but they were never the same again. The laughter returned to the house, but it was less jubilant. They were both fulfilling their previous duties but with a little less momentum. Mom lost her inner joy; her smile returned, but it no longer spanned from ear to ear.

Dad was stoic and resolved not to show his true feelings, as he thought the patriarch of the family should be. He was unable to hide his aging face that seemed to appear overnight. Even after the grieving period, those hard-set wrinkles didn't go away. I wonder if burying his feelings so deep is what caused his heart issues a year later. I'm not a doctor, but I do know that Dad's health declined abruptly after John's death. He may not have been the reason, but if emotional stress can damage your health, then John was partially to blame.

One morning Dad went to work as normal. The next morning, he and William went to Lexington for a scheduled heart catheterization. I remember being a little nervous but not overly concerned, because everyone else was hiding their worry from me. When Mom picked me up from school that day, I recognized the look on her face—she was worried. As we walked up the hill from the grade school, she tried to explain Dad's health condition to me, as well as you can explain it to a fourth grader. I stared at the gravel road and cried the rest of the way home.

That evening a friend from down the road came over to play. Normally Mom never said no, but she did that evening. We had to get up very early the next morning to make it to Lexington for Dad's triple bypass surgery. As I told my friend why I couldn't play that evening, I couldn't help but cry a little. Looking at me with sympathetic eyes and a frown, she opened our front porch gate and retreated down the steps.

Before bed Mom and I picked out a bright outfit with lime-green-and-black stripes for me to wear to the hospital. It practically glowed in the dark, so I knew the bright colors would cheer Dad up. Mom and I again were in a trance walking around the big empty house by ourselves. I was so worried that Mom and I would lose Dad. I couldn't fathom losing him and trying to piece our family back together again. We had already bonded over one death—we couldn't face another together.

After surgery the cardiologist would not release Dad to return to work. The backbreaking labor in the mines was more than Dad's heart could handle. That realization wasn't easy for Dad. He was a doer and a provider. He was heartbroken that returning to work wasn't an option, but he didn't wallow in his sadness—instead, he channeled it into doing other things. He started walking daily, building up his strength as the doctor recommended. Slowly he started cutting the grass in the flat areas of our yard. From there he started helping in the garden. Before long he was back to cutting his own grass and maintaining his garden without needing help.

CHAPTER 20

Growing Up with Grief

I was haunted by the images and sounds from the morning of his suicide. I was grieving before I even knew what grieving was.

Those early years after John passed away, there were a lot of lonely days for me, Mom, and Dad, especially during the holidays. Starting on Christmas Eve, I would pace from the living room window to the kitchen window, watching for company. We had family come in and out, but they couldn't stay long due to other family obligations. It was so hard to watch others pour into the house, sharing stories of where they had been and whose house they were going to next while we sat there alone.

Over the holidays we usually went to see Grandma Sparks, my maternal grandmother. Arriving at and leaving from Grandma's house, I would always look up on the hill where John was buried, but I rarely walked up there to visit. From the driveway, I could see the red flower arrangements that Mom had meticulously arranged and sent by Dad. She couldn't stand going to the graveyard, but she never missed sending flowers by Dad to decorate for Christmas and Memorial Day. I followed her lead and only visited the graveyard a handful of times while I was younger.

Grandma's big farmhouse was either frigid or blazing hot—there was no in-between. She had only a coal stove, two fireplaces, and a few wall heaters for her 15-room house. So, everyone migrated to the living room or kitchen where the fireplaces were blazing and the wall heaters were on high. That heat was too much for some to handle—you would find them sneaking outside or into the back of the house, but not me. I froze back then, so I always claimed a place close to the fire. Being around family made the holidays a little easier. The noise and commotion replaced the loneliness. The laughter and jokes made the holidays easier.

Once we were back at home, I would anxiously wait for William and Nicole to arrive so that we could eat dinner and open gifts. In a child's eyes, it seemed to take far longer to eat dinner than to open gifts. Nicole and I were anxious to see what was under the tree, and I believe the adults may have enjoyed making us wait, even just a little. Once we were all in the living room and the youngest child had started opening their gifts, I didn't mind waiting for my turn, because it allowed curiosity to build.

After all the presents were opened, all you could see were stacks of toys, clothes, and garbage bags filled with paper and bows. I knew once the mess was cleaned up that Nicole and William would be leaving. They both had other family members to visit on Christmas Eve, so they had to watch their time closely. For me, visitors were not there long enough. I hated it when they left because the excitement and anticipation were gone. The house was lonely and quiet once more. Even though I had just opened a lot of presents, I didn't feel happy and joyful. I played with my toys and loved them, but I was alone. When I was younger, I hated that quiet time after all the hustle and bustle of the holidays.

Under the sadness and confusion, there was a rage boiling inside of my heart. No matter the effort I put forth to quiet it, I couldn't. That rage kept rising until it blanketed my heart, only leaving a shell of who I was before. My life seemed darker and less magical than when I was a young child. I was playing with dolls one day and, the next, watching an ambulance gurney roll John out of the house with a single white sheet covering his body. Hearing the scream from Mom paired with the sight of the gurney left a lasting memory burned into my brain. During my deepest sadness, that memory is what I see first when thinking of him. I think of the moment he was wheeled from his childhood home because he chose to leave us.

I had to live in the home that John took his life in. Every day, I walked by the bedroom where he pulled the trigger. I watched Mom and Dad deteriorate in front of my eyes. I saw how the pain of losing John changed them individually and as a couple. For me, there was no escape from the sadness or memories.

I was the forgotten victim of John's suicide, the daughter who everyone assumed was fine. They were so wrong, and I was too young to adequately explain how I felt. I missed John and his booming laughter, his snide remarks and silly grin after saying something he shouldn't have.

I was haunted by the images and sounds from the morning of his suicide. I was grieving before I even knew what grieving was. Nightmares were coming so frequently that Mom had to sleep with me for a while. Did she know they were a result of John's death? Maybe. Maybe not. Is it fair of me to blame them on John's death? The old me would have said it wasn't. But after his death, I was grieving while awake and asleep. Mom tried her best to reassure me that the nightmares were not real and that I was safe. Yes, physically with her and Dad, I was safe. Mentally, I was broken!

I was one of the children judged by the faults of my birth parents. I felt the sting of words and saw the pitying faces that some people offered. What none of those people realized was that I had an amazing mom and dad who protected me and loved me. I was exposed very little to drinking, fighting, and partying. Other people didn't consider that at all; instead, it was easier to judge me.

I was treated differently because of who my family was, which was ridiculous. No child should ever be treated differently because of what their family may or may not have done. No one has the right to speak negatively about anyone else, so comments like "She will never amount to anything," or "She's not allowed to play with my kids," only show ignorance on the part of the speaker.

Insults and negativity would continue to swirl around me and my family in the years following John's death. During my eighth-grade year,

I was crowned football homecoming queen, which meant everything to me. Wearing that crown and hearing the cheers meant that I was worthy of friendship and positive things. That evening as I walked off the field, my smile spanned my entire face. Physically shaking from the adrenaline, I couldn't contain my excitement. With all the commotion from being crowned homecoming queen, I didn't think about my picture being taken for the annual. Evidently the person in charge of taking the picture didn't deem it important to take my picture either.

The photographer was good friends with one of the other contestants who wasn't happy about not winning. Did she not take my picture intentionally? I can't say for sure, but it did feel that way. The disgruntled classmate couldn't wait to tell me how unworthy I was of the crown and the title. She was furious that I had won and was certain that it had been rigged, which was absurd—it was an eighth-grade homecoming ceremony.

I wish I could say that her snide comment didn't affect me, but it did. It brought me back to the little girl who wasn't worthy, the little girl whom others either felt sorry for or made fun of. Looking for consolation, I went straight to Mom and told her what had been said. Before all the words left my mouth, I wish I hadn't told her. Her face drooped, and her eyes squinted as she stuttered over her words, trying to make me feel better.

I realized at that moment that she hurt more for me than I hurt for myself. I wished then that I could have taken the words back and not have burdened her with them. Unloading my pain onto her wasn't worth it. Even though she was hurt, she still found the energy to fight for me.

That's exactly what she did the next morning. We restyled my hair and applied fresh makeup. I slipped my black velvet dress back on and placed the crown on top of my head. Sitting in her blue chair, I held my one-day-old flowers and smiled brightly for the camera. The picture snapped that morning is the one that was used in the yearbook.

Believing that others wanted to be my friend was difficult for me. I couldn't see my own worth and struggled to believe that others would value my friendship. Those feelings made it difficult for me to allow others in and to share how I truly felt. One friendship that formed in middle school was exactly what I needed. We were polar opposites.

Stephanie was a beauty queen, cheerleader, and popular girl. I was reserved, negative, and poor, pitiful me. She was like a breath of fresh air; she didn't judge others or speak a negative word about anyone, even the people who deserved it. She had a way of letting the negativity go and focusing on the happiness. She was the exact type of person whom I needed in my life—that was God intervening.

After spending time at her home, I got to know her mom, and I understood where she got her love for others. Her mom was the mom who would greet you at the door with a big smile and hug, asking how your day was. She meant it; she really cared how you were doing. Her door was always open to company—we were not an inconvenience or a bother. She loved having us over to visit. Spending the night at her house meant late-night movies and snacks in the den. The next day her mom would take us to McDonald's for lunch. Both of us rode in the front seat together because it wasn't cool to ride in the back—sorry, officers. I didn't realize how much I enjoyed the little things in my childhood until I started writing this book.

The seeds that Stephanie planted in my 13-year-old heart took years to bloom, but she deserves a lot of the credit. She knew about my entire life story and still loved me. She used every opportunity to talk with me about God's love and acceptance. She always encouraged me to attend church with her or with anyone. I wasn't ready to act on those conversations yet, but they stayed with me until I was ready. She was a friend that God sent me at the right time in my life. Those summers at her house were exactly what I needed.

As I said, people flocked to her, so there were always other girls and guys around. It didn't matter how many people were there, she still made sure that everyone felt included. She had a gift! I became close friends with a few of the girls and realized there were more people like her in the world. I loved being around all of them because it was lighthearted and fun—no judgments or snide comments. From these friends I realized that you could be beautiful, popular, and genuinely kind. They were not insecure about who they were; therefore, they encouraged everyone to shine.

One afternoon on Stephanie's porch, Lea was squirming in her seat picking at her nails and not making eye contact with any of us. I assumed it was boy trouble because she was torn between two totally different guys. After a few tries of talking with her, I got the distinct impression that she did not want to talk to me, so I stopped. Feeling a little uncomfortable, I decided to call my parents to pick me up.

Before they arrived, Lea blurted out, "I am so sorry, Brandi. Mom said I could not be friends with you anymore."

Shocked, I asked, "What did I do?"

"It's because of who your brother is. Mom doesn't want me around David, or anyone connected with him."

My face felt as if it were on fire from the shock. My stomach was in knots pulling so tightly that I thought I would fall over from the pain. I stood there looking at her waiting for further explanation. I had no idea what my brother could have done to cause her mom to not like me.

Yes, he was wild and outspoken, and that's putting it mildly, but what did his actions have to do with me? We didn't even live together. The only time I saw him was when he came to my house to visit, and during those visits, he was on his best behavior—well, best behavior for him.

I left that evening feeling embarrassed. I was so tired of being judged for things out of my control. I was tired of others not seeing me for who I was. Instead, they were judging me based on family members that I didn't live with and only occasionally interacted with. I didn't tell Mom what was said. There was no need to hurt her more than what she already had been. There was nothing that she could have done to change the situation.

I worried that my friendship with Stephanie would change as well. The next time I went to her house, I was breathing a little harder and talking faster than normal. I kept my head down to not make eye contact, afraid of what would be said. Her mom wasted no time making me feel welcomed and loved. With a hug from her, my breathing slowed, and a smile formed. Stephanie and her mom were the type of people who made you want to be better.

I was fortunate to have two great friends who treated me like family. Heather and Stephanie's families showed me that I did have a place where I belonged. I was worthy of friendship and not judged by things out of my control. They were the kind of friends that a friend should be.

My lifelong best friend, Heather, was a true ally and supporter. Her friendship didn't waver no matter the circumstances. Heather's parents were always inclusive and welcoming to me. Her mother was the epitome of a great primary school teacher. She was loving and nurturing but strict. She had a love for reading that she passed on to her daughter—me, not so much then. I do love to read now and wonder if she planted a seed for it way back when. Before we were old enough to drive, she chauffeured us to the city pool or the movie theater all summer. She and Heather are the reasons I had so much fun over the summers. Heather's dad was funny and shared a love of watermelon with me. Occasionally he would send me some watermelon by Heather. To him, it wasn't anything special; to me, it meant a lot.

Maybe the parents realized they were showing me not everyone was judgmental, or maybe they were oblivious. Either way, I knew I wanted to be like them when I grew up. I wanted to include others and not be so fast to pass judgment. I wanted kids to have a chance to grow and prosper without the baggage of their families or supposed baggage of their families. Heather and Stephanie's families showed me there was a way.

CHAPTER 21

Buried Emotions

A consistent fear of saying the wrong thing inhibited me from sharing the barrage of feelings that were festering within my heart.

During the summer and fall months, Mom and I would sit on our blue swing and watch as the football team scrimmaged, the band practiced, and the cheerleaders performed stunts. The cheerleaders exuded grace and confidence with every movement. To me, that was the epitome of high school, and I fantasized about being a part of the team.

Standing on the porch facing our large picture window, I practiced my middle school cheers, envisioning myself as a high school varsity cheerleader. I was so engrossed in that daydream that I could feel the fall evening and see the day starting to turn into night as the fans in the bleachers cheered along with us. I pictured the game coming to an end as I stood below the hill waiting for my boyfriend to exit the locker room. Together we would walk into the dance and spend the rest of the evening together.

During middle school I enjoyed being a cheerleader, or at least the thought of it. I didn't have the drive to push myself beyond the basics such as taking gymnastics or perfecting my toe touches. Good enough was fine for me. Our school was small, so I didn't have a lot of competition. I'm not sure if they even cut kids from the team in middle school; if they did, I don't remember it.

Going into my freshman year, I tried out for the high school varsity squad, which to my surprise, I made. Excitement doesn't come close to describing how elated I was to be a member of a team that I had idolized since I was a child. Standing on those sidelines as a varsity high school cheerleader meant that I had made it. I was someone who did have value and deserved to be a part of the team. It was a short-term confidence booster that I needed to start high school on a high note.

Summer was winding down, and it was finally time to attend my first summer cheer camp, like so many I had watched before. This time I was wearing black cheer shorts and a white cheerleading shirt, like every other girl on the squad. I wasn't standing on the porch pretending to be a cheerleader; I was one. It was a surreal time for me, being a part of something bigger than myself. I wanted nothing more than to stand on the sidelines with like-minded females and forge new friendships that would last throughout high school and beyond.

My excitement waned faster than I ever anticipated. By midseason I was dreading practice and games. By the end of the day, I had no energy left to give. All I wanted to do was go home and lie down on the couch. The amount of effort that it took for me to go to school, interact with friends, and go to practice left me mentally and physically drained. I was constantly in a bad mood because I had nothing else left to give.

I had no idea what depression was or that I was suffering with it as a child. I don't think others around me realized it either. I believe some of the adults thought I was lazy and a slacker, while others like my parents were just happy I was staying out of trouble. They couldn't see my depression, because to them depression wasn't real. Mom nor Dad ever talked about depression or the need for any type of mental health. It wasn't until I went to counseling as an adult, that I realized how drastically depression affected my childhood.

I often pretended to be sick so that I didn't have to go to school or practice. Sometimes Mom let me miss; other times, she made me go. I believe in some ways she felt sorry for me. Attending school and cheer practice was physically too much for me. I was fatigued and disengaged. Faking it for so long around others was exhausting. I didn't want them to see me sad or ridden with anxiety. After exerting the level of energy that it took to hide those emotions, I had nothing left to give. I watched other friends go to school and participate in extracurricular activities without any effort. I couldn't fathom why I was so lazy and unmotivated compared to others.

By the end of the season, I had no intention of trying out for the cheerleading squad the following year. I was officially through with it. At the time I didn't see anything wrong with me not returning to the squad. After all, I had fulfilled my one-year obligation. I wish the adult me could have told the child me to stick with it, even if it was hard.

Dropping out of extracurriculars and doing good enough in school set a precedent in my early years. I thought it was okay to give up if things were too hard. I didn't believe in pushing myself to be successful. The fear of failure was constantly in the back of my mind. If I put in real effort and wasn't successful, I thought I would be seen as a failure.

Instead of talking with someone about my struggles, I just accepted it as my lot in life. I put in minimal effort and maintained a safe boundary between myself and the potential for failure. There were so many things that I wanted to accomplish, but I didn't have the sticking power to see them through. Instead, once it got hard, I pulled back as if I hadn't even tried.

Staying on the cheerleading team would have helped me to grow and possibly rescued me from more years of the ho-hum attitude. Looking back at myself, I am furious—furious that someone didn't notice that I needed help, furious that I didn't ask for it sooner. Maybe had I been honest about how I truly felt, my life would have been different.

Depression had cast a gray net over my entire life; the lens through which I viewed life was bleak. I felt unwanted. My biological mother had given me away but kept her other kids. My birth father committed suicide in the home I lived in because I didn't listen.

I was carrying a heavy weight that others didn't see or know about, because I feared my sadness would be too much for Mom to bear. I kept my feelings to myself and didn't dare broach them with anyone else as a child.

I had so many questions that I didn't feel comfortable asking. I needed reassurance that it wasn't my fault that John died, but how could I possibly ask for that when Mom and Dad were in so much pain? Talking about him with Mom or Dad felt unfair. To talk about John with an outsider felt like betrayal—and at the time, therapy for grief and loss was unheard of. Oh, how I changed in those early years.

My subconscious replayed the redundant phrases that I heard during the funeral:

"Your mom and dad are going to need you to be there for them."

Or, "Your mom and dad are going to need you to be good."

Or, "They are going to need you to be strong for them."

What well-intentioned family and friends didn't realize is the value I placed on those statements and the influence they grew to have on my life. Maybe I would have felt the same way about my parents with or without those comments. I am still very overprotective of my parents' legacy. To me, it doesn't matter if they were right or wrong; I was always on Mom's side. I felt a deep connection to Mom and her happiness, to the point that it was my mission to protect her and love her no matter what the future held.

I struggled to reconcile my thoughts without voicing them to anyone. A consistent fear of saying the wrong thing inhibited me from sharing the barrage of feelings that were festering within my heart. My thoughts and interactions became guarded without intention. I repeated phrases that I heard others say about John and death, or I sat quietly and listened to others as they spoke. As a child, I was missing my biological father, but I was also angry at him. I didn't feel comfortable sharing my feelings of anger or confusion with Mom because she was suffering enough. I didn't want to add further worry or sadness to her already broken heart.

At first, she couldn't talk about John without crying. With the mere mention of his name, she would bite the tip of her tongue as a mechanism to hold back the tears. Even behind her thick glasses, I could see her eyes gloss over with tears on the verge of spilling over. How could I ever let her know that I was angry at John for what he did to her and Dad? I wanted her to see me as an ally, one who was on her side, who viewed John as she did.

So, I was the good daughter, the one who referred to John as "Big Daddy"—the name that I had always called him since I was a baby—because Mom needed to hear that, not because I felt he deserved it. Voicing my anger would have placed Mom between two children. To defend one would be to stand against the other. No parent should have to pick sides between their children. Expressing my true feelings was not worth the pain that it would cause her.

I didn't think he deserved the title Big Daddy, because a daddy would never hurt a child in such a way. They wouldn't allow their child and mother to see them take their own life. They wouldn't take their own life in the house that the daughter he had already given away for adoption had to live in. That was another point of my anger. Mom and Dad had to walk by that room every day—the room that their son shot himself in. How do you do that to your parents?

On that cold November morning, John took a piece of me with him. I lost the fun and silly childhood that I deserved. The lightheartedness and safety that a child should feel at home were erased. A happy mom who belly laughed was gone. A dad who played with me in the yard was gone. They were both there and still trying their best, but I saw the distant stares, the tears, and the pain that they felt. They pushed themselves as hard as they could for me.

I loved them both more than anything in this world because I knew firsthand what they were going through. I lived it in real time with them. Until you are there day in and day out, you can't understand what a family goes through after that type of trauma.

I was angry at John for hurting them so deeply and completely. His life wasn't the only life that ended with the pull of the trigger—the life we, his family, had known ended as well. That morning was hell for us. The tears were so heavy and constant that I couldn't keep my face dry. My nose was red from rubbing it, but I still stood there in that doorframe and begged him to stay with us. I believed him when he said that he wouldn't do it and that he was sorry.

I felt relief that the nightmare was over and that John was going to be okay. The family dynamic seemed to be going back into familiar territory, with Mom fixing breakfast for him as she had so many mornings. I didn't fully trust him when he told me to go help Mom carry his food upstairs. I walked away from the bedroom reluctantly, not certain which person to listen to, Mom who said not to leave him or John who said to go help Mom. I walked away from the bedroom door because I thought the crisis had been adverted, that John was going to eat and sober up like so many times before. I ultimately chose to trust him and that cost him his life. Or did it?

Would he have shot himself in front of me? Would he have accidentally shot me? Would he have done it later that day? Or another day? All these questions flow through my mind every time I think of John. Did he intend to deceive me and Mom when he told us he had changed his mind?

Did Mom believe that he wasn't going to shoot himself? Or is that why she told me not to leave him? Was she trusting me to keep him alive, and I failed? Is my decision the one that changed everything?

My answers to these questions change depending on the mood I am in. I still waffle back and forth over the man he was, the man I thought he was, and the man I wanted him to be, when in reality he was a little of each. Accepting that I will never have an answer to these questions isn't easy for me. You see, I am someone who operates in definitive answers when it comes to those I love or the things I am passionate about. I'm not usually comfortable in the gray, unknown world.

CHAPTER 22
The Hidden Truth

I wore beautiful sequin dresses, rode on shiny sports cars,
waved during parades, and walked onto the basketball
court as if my life were perfect. Most of the people watching
me had no idea how I really felt about myself.

During the summer of my junior year, Mom and I were sitting on the front porch swing gazing at her rose bushes in the front yard. Those bushes had been nurtured and cared for by Mom and William for years—the roses were standing tall and thick with a metal rod supporting their weight. The roses had been the subject of several arguments between Mom and Dad during the mowing season. Dad, either hurrying to finish mowing or not paying attention, damaged those perfect flowers a few times. Mom was always fast to point out the damage and scold Dad in a playful yet semiserious way.

For as long as I can remember, Mom always had flower beds and pots placed around the yard and porch. Playing on the swing set or in the backyard, I caught glimpses of Mom weeding or watering the flower beds. I don't recall her working in them very often after John's death. It seems maybe William took over that role. I wonder if Mom lost her love for flowers and gardening because of depression or if she enjoyed seeing the final product no matter who did the work.

Our large wraparound front porch offered a steady breeze and melody from Mom's wind chime collection. They were strategically placed near

Mom's side of the porch. I am not sure why, because you could hear them from any point on the porch or even inside for that matter. She loved them, and Dad tolerated them. It was funny to see her give him a sly smile when the wind was really blowing through the porch. Dad would always shake his head and laugh. There was still a playful side between the two of them, but it wasn't something that was seen on a regular basis any longer. I didn't realize it at the time, but subconsciously, I was storing those memories of them being happy together.

That old porch swing may have changed colors throughout the years, and it shows more wear and tear today, but it is still one of the most significant pieces I have from my parents' home. Sitting on that swing with Mom, we had thousands, if not millions, of conversations over the years. During warmer months we spent more time there than anywhere else in the house. Sitting on that swing is where Mom told me I was adopted and that I had other brothers and sisters. On that swing is where Mom and I talked about Dad's bypass surgery. As I lay across that swing with my head in Mom's lap, she used a bobby pin to pull blackheads out of my nose. If you haven't experienced that type of pain, I don't recommend starting now. That swing is where Mom asked me if I wanted to go to Florida on vacation with William. Of course, the answer was yes, but I think Mom was hoping I would say no. She was worried about me going so far away without her, even though she knew I would be safe.

Between the sounds of the wind chimes and buzzing of the bees, our conversation twisted in and out of several topics till it stopped on John. She lit up a cigarette and then lightly bit the front of her tongue as she did when she was trying not to cry. I wanted her to know that she could talk to me about how she felt without feeling guilty. She was my best friend, even when I was 16. I sat there for a minute as I tried to decide how to broach the question that was burning in my mind. I finally realized there was no soft way to ask, so I turned my head toward Mom and asked, "Are you okay after losing John?" It was an elementary way to ask such a loaded question, but at 16 that was all I had.

She sat there quietly for a few minutes before responding, "The pain is still as raw today as it was the day it happened. I still question what I could have done differently, how I could have protected him from himself."

My eyes filled with tears as I said, "Mom, no one loved or protected him more than you."

With a sad grin and hunched shoulders, she said, "You know he was a good man, but the alcohol changed him. So many people have forgotten the good side of John."

Those words have stayed with me since that conversation. I realized that she would always see the John who was filled with goodness and laughter, the one who helped others and worked hard. He was her baby, and even though she couldn't save him, she would save his memory, even if for herself. She refused to see the son with alcohol issues, the son who hurt others, including her. Yes, she covered for him because she loved him. I get it. I am a mom, too, and I would probably protect my child at all costs.

When I was a teenager, listening to Mom talk about her feelings changed me in a way that I didn't understand at the time. I cried for her, not myself. I saw how much pain and guilt she carried around about John, and I prayed that I could take that away from her. As heartbroken as I was for her, I was angry at John for causing her and everyone else so much pain.

It hurt me to watch my parents suffer and agonize over John. They tried everything in their power to give him the help and support he needed. Counseling was not widely accepted, and dirty laundry was not aired for others to gossip about. My parents were operating without the help of experts to guide their way. I wonder if help would have been readily available and not frowned upon if things had been different. I wonder if someone could have interceded and changed John's trajectory or if it was too late. So many are fast to harshly judge the person suffering from addiction without thinking of why the addiction began.

I didn't realize it at the time, but I was adding more stress to Mom and Dad because of my own depression. After all the times faking sick, I was finally faced with a legitimate illness that caused abrupt pain. During the winter of my junior year, I wasn't faking it when I doubled over in pain. This time every symptom was real and as uncomfortable as I said it was. My family doctor referred me to a surgeon in Whitesburg, suspecting a bowel blockage. After I was admitted to the hospital the doctor ran several tests, and a bowel blockage was ruled out, but the pelvic ultrasound showed a large ovarian cyst. After consulting with an ob-gyn, it was determined that I would require surgery to remove the cyst on the following Monday. This was on a Thursday, and the doctor recommended keeping me in the hospital as a precaution in fear the cyst may rupture.

For a junior in high school focused on a weekend of basketball and homecoming festivities, staying in the hospital wasn't an option. Homecoming was so much more to me than a silly high school event—my self-worth was largely based on it. I felt chosen, and for a girl who didn't believe she was worthy of being kept, it served as a temporary morale booster.

I wore beautiful sequin dresses, rode on shiny sports cars, waved during parades, and walked onto the basketball court as if my life were perfect. Most of the people watching me had no idea how I really felt about myself. The bulk of the ridicule only lasted from early grade school to the end of middle school. Once I was in high school, my past or family was rarely mentioned. Unfortunately, from that point I didn't need a reminder of my early years. My own self-consciousness did that for me.

Being on the homecoming court also ensured that my hair and make-up were both done professionally. I did not have the ability to curl and tease my bangs like other girls did. My bangs either had a crimp where there should have been a curl, or they just fell flat. For those of you who had big hair in the early '80s, you know the hairstyle I am referring to: the teased-up bangs that resembled a rooster.

Missing homecoming was not an option for me. I didn't care about the potential consequences or pain. So, I begged Mom to allow me to still participate in the homecoming court. After a lot of convincing, I was allowed to go home and participate in homecoming only, not to watch the game or attend the dance. I arrived a few minutes before we walked on the court and left as soon as it was over. I spent the rest of the weekend on the couch, watching TV. It's amazing at that age how you can truly push your fears aside with a simple distraction. I didn't worry about the surgery on Friday or Saturday because I was focused on homecoming, but by Sunday evening, I was feeling nervous and uneasy.

Anxious and unable to sleep, I was curled up on the couch reading a teen magazine until the wee hours of Monday morning. The dim light and silence were not helping my anxiety. In fact, they were increasing it. The thought of being placed under anesthesia was terrifying to me. What if I didn't wake up? What if I had a reaction? All these questions were circling around in my head. I worried about death, because when you're raised by parents in a generation above your birth parents, you see a lot of death. I attended more funerals in my younger years than I can count. People who were once my great-aunts and great-uncles were converted to my aunts and uncles because of adoption. I lost a lot of people earlier than most. So, knowing how common death was, I feared I would be next. Of course, I didn't tell anyone else that. I didn't want anyone else to worry more than they already were.

William had been at Lynn's that evening and came home to me awake on the couch. Instead of going to bed, as I'm sure he had intended, he sat down in Dad's recliner and picked up the *Mountain Eagle*, our hometown newspaper, to read. After a few minutes of reading, he asked if I wanted anything to eat, but it was already past midnight. After realizing how late it was, he encouraged me to get some sleep. I knew he was exhausted, but he wasn't going to bed until I did. So, for him I snuggled under my covers and closed my eyes, giving way to the fatigue.

William took on the role of a partial father figure from the time I was a baby. I imagine that he felt a sense of responsibility to help care for me, both as John's older brother and as a help to his parents. His daughter, Nicole, was born nine months after me, so maybe he thought of her and how he hoped that someone would help take care of her if the roles were reversed. Either way, he was always there for me.

On Monday morning I checked into Whitesburg Appalachian Regional Healthcare for surgery with Mom, Dad, and William in the waiting room. The first procedure didn't go as planned—the surgeon was not able to reach the cyst by the small incision, so they had to do a different surgical procedure that required a much larger incision at the bottom of my abdomen.

After surgery I spent several days in the hospital, but I was rarely alone. Between Mom and William, one of them was always there by my side. Dad came in to visit and drive Mom to and from the hospital, but he wasn't the type to stay there with me. Hospitals made him nervous, so he avoided them at all costs.

I spent several weeks at home recovering before returning to school. It was boring and lonely watching all my friends continue with their lives as I sat on the couch. My parents knew I was struggling with being cooped up in the house all day, every day. After the news went off at seven, all of us loaded up into the white Ford Tempo and went to Dairy Queen for a Blizzard. This was a big deal, because Dad didn't believe in wasting gas or going out when it wasn't necessary, but for those few weeks, he made an exception. I looked forward to that nightly outing—it's what got me through the boring days.

CHAPTER 23

Impostor Syndrome

My inner thoughts became my reality.

Self-sabotage was my mantra. I spent years wallowing in self-doubt, anger, and depression. I wanted to play the victim instead of the victor. Being the victim allowed me to hide behind excuses instead of trudging forward. It wasn't easy to pull myself out of years of negativity. I struggled with the highs and lows and wondered if they would ever even out. It felt as if I were on a roller coaster, rising toward the top and speeding down the hill toward another failure.

The desire to be visible and invisible simultaneously was unrealistic and impossible to achieve; therefore, I set myself up for failure from an early age. I desired to be a part of something, to have a place among those with a purpose and goals, but I also wanted to shield myself from the prying eyes of others. So, I would shrink and mute myself to disappear into the background, only to desire inclusion and acknowledgment.

I think of all the dreams I had as a child, dreams that would have been attainable if I had only applied myself. But, for whatever reason, I couldn't do it. For example, I wanted to feel worthy of friendships. I wanted to be an honor student. I wanted to cheer for my football team as a varsity cheerleader, but the desire to do so couldn't overcome my lack of energy.

I had impostor syndrome. I felt unworthy of being friends with most people I socialized with. I was waiting for them to realize what a loser I was and to walk away. That feeling of waiting for the ax to drop was exhausting.

The anxiety that stemmed from potentially wearing the wrong clothes or saying the wrong thing was almost paralyzing. I felt I had to be just like other kids to be accepted. I was the unpopular kid who made the right friends or had the right family in the popular clique. That's what secured me a place, not my own merit but pity or obligation.

Nicole, my niece and William's daughter, had grown up with most of those girls and had the self-confidence and looks to secure her place within the group. Even though I was the older of the two, I wished to be more like her. She carried herself with confidence and grace, no matter what the situation. Her tall, slender frame demanded attention when she entered the room. Her fair skin and piercing blue eyes were not easy to forget. Her confidence didn't stem from looks alone; she was also intelligent. It seemed easy for her to excel in school. The plans for her future were not shadowed by doubt or "I can't." She knew she would. That's what I admired the most—that she always knew her worth.

Nicole was like a sister to me. With nine months between us, we were the perfect playmates. As children, we played with Barbies, baby dolls, and dress-up clothes. One of our favorite activities was a buzzer game that drove Mom crazy. We would beg to play repeatedly until the buzzers no longer worked. We played the game so often that we memorized all the answers but kept asking to play. We constantly fought over who won the game—it was indeed a sibling dynamic.

As teenagers, we did some silly things together that we would have only done with each other, probably because anyone else would have said we were crazy. At one point, we decided to spy on one of our ex-boyfriends. I won't say which one to maintain some secrecy and deniability. Nicole drove, and I rode in the passenger seat, using a baseball hat as a disguise. I don't remember if the ex-boyfriend saw us or not, but I am pretty sure he would have known it was me in a hat.

When the boy phase hit, we almost drove William crazy during one vacation. There was a group of hot boys staying at the same condo as we were. We did our best to flirt with them without being overly obvious.

Well, as overly obvious as two teenage girls could be. I can imagine what William thought as we acted so grown up—total face-palm moment here. It didn't take long for us to get in trouble with him. The boys came over to our balcony and tried to talk to us. If I remember right, they threw something up at us, and William heard it. Let's just say, Nicole and I spent the rest of the week with our heads down, embarrassed.

Nicole and I spent many summer vacations together on the beach or lake, inseparable for most of our childhood and youth. Our relationship was the closest I had to a real sister. After I was older, as a preteen and teenager, I started to wonder if she preferred not to hang out with me but didn't have a choice—not because she ever said anything, just simply because I doubted myself. That was unfair to her and the bond we had.

My other connection to the clique was my longtime best friend, Heather. We formed a fast and loyal friendship in kindergarten. She was a phenomenal basketball player with confidence and a sense of humor that made her liked by everyone. Standing over six feet tall, she had a presence when she entered the room. Actually, her laughter or sarcasm would be heard before she was seen, which everyone loved. Heather was devoted to a fault. She had perfect attendance from grade school through high school. She came to school sick, tired, and during emergencies—you name it, she was there. I can remember times when she was so sick in class that it looked as if she would fall over, but she pushed through. Her grades were another example of her grit. She was our class valedictorian. I was proud to be her best friend.

When I was really rolling around in my negativity, I would make ridiculous comments like "Heather would not have been my friend had we not met so young." Maybe that wasn't the truth, but I thought it at the time. That comment didn't give Heather the justice that she deserved. I was selling our friendship short.

I regretted not staying on the cheerleading squad during my senior year, so I tried out for the team again. On the days leading up to the tryouts, I repeatedly told myself I wasn't good enough to make the squad. My jumps weren't as high as the other competitors'. I couldn't do any substantial flips. I hadn't practiced a cheer or dance routine in three years. I was entirely out of my league. My inner thoughts became my reality. I didn't make the cheerleading squad. I didn't deserve to make it either.

I had already convinced myself that I wasn't good enough. So, instead of practicing more or asking for help, I just approached it with an I-don't-care attitude. I'm sure the judges could sense my lackadaisical attitude when I walked out on the floor. I didn't show confidence or excitement; in fact, I acted as if I didn't really want to be there.

I was humiliated over not making the squad. That single piece of paper posted in the hallway was like a knife stabbing through my gut. I was angry and embarrassed. I blamed the coach for my failure. I told myself I didn't get chosen because she didn't like me. Anything that saved my reputation is what I clung to. It had to be anyone else's fault but mine.

Looking back on that situation now, I understand that I was the reason I didn't make the squad. I didn't put forth the effort or enthusiasm that the tryout deserved. I allowed my negativity to hamper my ability. I told myself I wasn't good enough, so guess what? I wasn't. I wasn't used to losing because I didn't put myself in a situation to fail. So, that defeat was uncharted territory for me.

I struggled with a lack of interest and energy for as long as I can remember. By the end of the school day, I was depleted, with nothing else left to give. Getting ready for school was such a chore for me. Doing homework after school was a consistent fight. All I wanted to do was lie on the couch and nap. I constantly complained of being exhausted with no energy. I was always asking to miss school because I was sick. I had more pretend sinus infections than I can even remember.

Mom wanted to believe me, and instead of calling my bluff, she often let me stay home. I'm sure, on some level, she knew I was exaggerating my symptoms to stay home, but she didn't push me. She finally told the doctor that I was exhausted and sick all the time and that I couldn't seem to get my energy back. The doctor suggested it could be mono or a vitamin deficiency. I don't remember having blood work done, but I do remember starting weekly vitamin B_{12} injections for a month. After four weekly injections, the doctor decreased it to monthly. I don't know how long I took the injections, but they didn't help. Finally, Mom agreed to let me stop taking them. After that, my lack of energy was no longer addressed.

When I was a student, my grades hovered between a B and C average, not because I wasn't smart but because I *believed* I wasn't. I would repeatedly make comments like "There is no way I will ever learn this," or "I'm not capable of doing any better than I am." It was easier to fantasize than to put in the work to do it. My grades were average, mostly Bs and Cs. It didn't matter the amount of effort I put in because my levels of comprehension and retention were the same. I could not comprehend most of what I read, even if I read it more than once, which didn't happen often. It didn't matter if the room was completely quiet without any distractions or if the room was filled with commotion.

The constant wandering of my mind prevented me from retaining what I was reading. Listening to a teacher in class was torture to me. Instead, my focus was easily disrupted by my own thoughts saying, you will never be able to do this. I was selling myself short because I lacked confidence in my abilities.

Of course, I couldn't do it because I didn't give myself the chance to learn it. I just assumed I was unable to comprehend it and turned off the desire to try. I couldn't understand why other people seemed to retain the information and find school easy, while I struggled. Maybe had I not missed school so frequently, the material would have been easier to understand. Maybe had I tried harder or asked for help, I would have done better.

My parents were proud of me no matter what. I could have brought home an A or a C; it didn't matter to them. They were simply happy I was alive and staying out of trouble. As I got older, we talked about college. I knew that I would go because that's what was expected: a four-year degree and a career.

CHAPTER 24
Ready for Change

*I knew I had to change the direction of my
life, or I would never be happy.*

When I started filling out college applications, my high school guidance counselor was surprised by my interest. She was always a little intimidating and very direct during any conversation. So, when she called me into her office to discuss my college options, I was nervous. Sitting at her desk, she thumbed through my high school transcript with a shocked expression. Her raised eyebrows and deep breaths served only to increase my anxiety. After completing her review, she looked me squarely in the eyes and said, "I didn't realize you wanted to go to college. Your grades are average, but your attendance is poor. I feel like you do not have the structure or basic foundation to be successful at a four-year institution. If you are certain that you would like to attend college, I recommend a community college for the first two years."

I sat there with my eyes wide and a bitter taste in my mouth, trying to formulate a response to her, but nothing came out.

She prompted me again, "What do you think of that, Brandi?"

I muttered, "I will try harder in college. I have to go to Clinch Valley College."

"Brandi, I don't think that is a good idea, but I will help you get your application ready."

"Okay, thank you," I whispered as I stood up. I left her office without discussing the next steps or deadlines. I just wanted out of that situation. Whom did she think she was telling me that I wasn't ready for college? I couldn't wait to tell Mom—I knew she would talk to my guidance counselor and fix everything.

Mom was as angry as I was when I told her about the conversation, so angry that she met with my guidance counselor the next morning. I don't know what was said, because I wasn't in the meeting. All I know was that my guidance counselor gave me everything I needed to apply to Clinch Valley. That evening Mom and I sat down at the kitchen table and completed my application. We enclosed all the necessary test scores and transcripts with smiles on our faces.

I didn't choose Clinch Valley College because of its curriculum, even though it was a good school. I chose it because of its proximity to my family. William lived in Wise, less than 10 minutes from the college campus. It was approximately 40 minutes from Mom and Dad. I could see my brother during the week and my mom and dad every weekend. What solidified my decision was knowing that Heather, my best friend since kindergarten, was also going to Clinch Valley.

Graduation was only a few weeks away, and I was filled with nervous energy. Had I made the right decision about college? Was I smart enough to go? Could I leave Mom? Questions such as those haunted me every day. I could tell that Mom was emotional over my graduation as well. She was proud but also sad and worried. I'm still not certain whether she felt that way because I was her little girl and she was going to miss me when I was gone or if she was worried that my guidance counselor was correct about my ability to go to Clinch Valley.

Either way, she planned a graduation party for me. She busied herself cleaning the house and cooking all my favorite foods several days before the party. Mom handled the guest list with just suggestions from me. Of course, William, Lynn, and Nicole were invited and my aunts and uncles who lived close by. All my friends would be celebrating with their families, so it was a small family party, which I loved the idea of.

I would be remiss if I didn't admit there was a sadness looming over my graduation. I wanted John to be there with us, to celebrate as a family. One evening I sat down across from Mom in her sitting room and asked, "Do you think John would be proud of me?"

A sad smile formed across her face as she said, "Of course, he would have—he is proud of you."

"Proud of you" just hung in the silence as we both sat there staring at the TV.

"What about Karen?" I asked.

Mom responded, "I know she is too."

"Do you think she would come to my graduation party?" I softly stuttered.

"Well, Brandi, I believe so. Do you want to invite her?"

"Yeah, is that okay?"

"Of course, it is," Mom responded without hesitation.

I was apprehensive to invite Karen myself, so Mom did it for me. Realistically, she probably should have made me extend the invitation, but I think she saw I was too nervous. Subconsciously, I was afraid of being rejected by Karen. So I used Mom as a buffer between me and Karen. Mom and Karen still talked on the phone, so it wasn't out of the norm for one to call the other on occasion. When Mom reported back to me that she was going to try and make it, I was ecstatic and nervous.

I didn't see Karen until after my graduation. There she stood on the back left side of the bleachers with a bouquet of flowers. She was smiling proudly and talking to Mom. When I approached, we were both nervous. My brain was racing, trying to decide what to say and how to say it. I was intimidated by her, not because she had ever done anything to make me feel that way. She was just this person out of reach for me, someone I didn't know. She handed me the flowers, stared me straight in the eyes, and said, "I am proud of you." At that moment, "I am proud of you" meant more than anything else she could have said to me.

I started my freshman year at Clinch Valley College with the goal of becoming a psychologist or psychiatrist. I could envision all the individuals whom I would help and the lives that I would change. What I couldn't envision was the level of effort that degree required. After realizing the classes were harder than I expected them to be, I started skipping classes to work additional shifts.

My guidance counselor was correct—I wasn't ready for college coursework. I didn't graduate from Clinch Valley. Instead, I decreased my load to a part-time student so I could work. As a part-time student, I was less devoted to my classes than I was as a full-time student. So, I decided to take a semester off. That semester off lasted for several years.

During the hiatus from college, I married my first husband, and we had our son Braden. My husband and I were married for approximately six years before an amicable separation and divorce. As friends, we coparent Braden without issues.

In 2008 I started to realize that so many of the things that went wrong in my life were my fault. I didn't take responsibility for my actions or lack thereof. I knew I had to stop making excuses and blaming my actions on my childhood.

I knew that I couldn't overcome all my issues without help, so I finally heeded the advice of others and scheduled an appointment with a counselor. My apprehension grew exponentially during the week of my first appointment. Self-doubt was even interfering with my desire to get help. Would she think I was crazy? Would she tell me I had no reason to feel the way I do? Would she tell me there was nothing she could do to help me?

I loathed the expression "It's never too late to start." I would think, It's easy for you to say that. You're not the kid who was given away for adoption. You're not the kid who saw her birth father commit suicide. You're not a new single mom barely making it. Or whatever excuse that came to my mind—trust me, I had a lot of them. I used those phrases as a crutch to prevent me from having to try. I wasn't happy or satisfied. I was continually beating myself up over my failures.

I knew I had to change the direction of my life, or I would never be happy. So, I took a big leap in 2010. I applied to and was accepted into King University's online Bachelor of Business Administration (BBA) program. It seemed like the worst time to return to school. I was a single mother who worked full-time, and I was in a new relationship. My time was already extremely limited, but I knew it had to be then.

The accelerated BBA program was time consuming and overwhelming at times. A new class started every six weeks, so missing one assignment or slacking for a week wasn't an option. I had to develop time management skills and set schedules that I didn't deviate from to keep everything moving smoothly, and even then, things still got off track occasionally. It was up to me to get the laundry done, feed myself and my son, Braden, and make sure that Braden was cared for and participated in his extracurricular activities. There were times that I felt as if the world was resting on my shoulders and that I couldn't do it all.

More times than I can count, I cried at my kitchen table because I felt as if I were a failure. I would read and reread chapters and still not understand the text. I had to teach myself how to study and develop a program for myself on how to retain and understand the information I was reading. Even though I was facing obstacle after obstacle, I was prouder of myself than I had been in my entire life. I had made a commitment to completing my bachelor's degree, and with the completion of every six weeks, I was getting closer.

Graduation day was a milestone for me that was incomparable to anything else I have ever accomplished. Almost 10 years after my first attempt at college, I graduated. Completing my degree changed my life trajectory—I proved to myself that I was capable.

I'm grateful for what I have accomplished since being a scared, timid child hiding behind others. I'm proud of the me I am now. I am proud that I didn't allow my past to dictate my future. You can be proud of yourself too. Your past does not have any place in your future. You can change the course at any time.

The only boundaries that held me back were the ones I created. Don't allow yourself to be held back because of fear. Instead, stare it in the face and push forward. Now, start dreaming. Start identifying your wins. Start checking off those accomplishments.

CHAPTER 25
Accepting the Unknown

I struggled to stand up for myself in fear
of making someone else leave.

Unanswered questions caused me to grow up looking for a sense of belonging and purpose that escaped me as a child. The gnawing question of why my birth parents didn't raise me took up permanent residence in my mind. They each kept and raised their other children—I was the only one given away for adoption. Was I not good enough? Did I remind them of a time they wanted to forget?

Focusing on my inability to be loved by my birth parents, I assumed I was unworthy of love from others. My detrimental mindset caused years of heartache and confusion that were unnecessary and unhealthy, not just for myself but everyone intertwined in my life.

The unknown answers distorted me into someone I didn't like, someone who was fake and insecure, who looked to others for guidance and support. I struggled to stand up for myself in fear of making someone else leave. I grew up imitating others instead of being my true self. I couldn't risk alienating someone else because I didn't act the way they thought I should. For years that was who I was, the person who would change into whoever she needed to be to fit into that situation—someone who stood out enough to be noticed but not enough to leave an impression.

I don't feel that it's fair to blame my self-doubt, insecurities, and un-trusting tendencies on John's death, but that's when it all began. How could I trust anyone completely after he lied to me, saying that he would not take his own life, only to turn around and do it a short time later? I didn't share this sentiment with anyone for years because I was protecting the memory and integrity of my family. I felt as if I were disgracing him by sharing how his actions affected me.

The parents who raised me—my grandparents—were doting, lov-ing, and trustworthy—truly everything I needed or wanted in parents. I have heard that grandparents are more understanding and lenient with the grandchildren they raise, and that was true in my case. I was Daddy's doll and Mom's world from the minute they held me.

For all intents and purposes, my family was amazing. I was blessed with two parents who were always there for me, an older brother, William, who was like a second dad, and a niece, Nicole, who was like a sister. The amount of love that I received from that small group is more love than oth-ers may feel in an entire lifetime.

But even so, there was something still missing, something unfulfilled. I wanted this other family that was mysterious and out of reach. More importantly, I wanted them to want me.

I remember a brief glimpse of Mom telling me I was adopted. It's more like a snapshot frozen in my memory. I was a young child, with brown hair hanging in my face, matted from the sweat of playing outside. I was standing in front of the swing, facing Mom, her feet planted on the porch, not allowing the swing to move as we talked. It was just her and me on the porch. She told me that John and Karen were my birth parents, but she and Dad were my real parents. When I was a little baby, they decided they wanted to raise me as their own and had loved me like that ever since.

That simple explanation was how I was first introduced to my adop-tion. There wasn't any negativity or focus on why I was adopted. Mom kept the explanation simple and direct. At the time what she said didn't faze me. I didn't have any other questions or need additional information.

She did a wonderful job of normalizing my adoption in such a way that I didn't feel different from other kids. As a young child, I thought my family was no different from any of my friends' families. I had no idea that most kids didn't have a Big Daddy (John), a birth mom, and parents. Everyone around me operated as if nothing was out of the norm. So I did as well. I referred to John as Big Daddy and my dad (paternal grandfather) as dad.

Once I started school, I realized that my family tree wasn't the norm, and my thoughts began to change. It was a hard realization to accept that birth parents didn't just give their kids away, that parents loved and raised their children, even if they weren't together. Divorce and separation dictated who the child lived with, but typically they stayed with one of their birth parents.

Some of my friends and classmates lived in broken homes or stayed with their grandparent's part of the time, but their grandparents weren't their mom and dad. Their parents didn't give them away. I couldn't understand why I was so different. They couldn't understand it either and often told me as much.

All those youthful emotions and hormones running through my mind and body, paired with unanswered questions, left me an emotional wreck. I was envious of my brothers and sisters because our birth parents chose to keep them. I was envious of friends who grew up with siblings. The negative self-talk was compounded with self-doubt and jealousy. All those feelings led to and intensified my guilt for being ungrateful.

I felt as if I were living in two different universes, fighting with myself on which family I belonged with. I craved the family I didn't have but loved the family I had. I didn't know if my feelings were justifiable and normal or if I was being selfish. So I kept them to myself. What good would it have done to hurt anyone else?

During my teen years, I began to understand how addiction and alcohol changed my trajectory. That realization evoked anger and confusion. Not knowing why things happened the way they did was difficult. Operating in a world of assumptions and best guesses left room for doubt and what ifs. I could have asked my mom about my adoption, but I didn't want to dredge up painful memories. For her to explain why John gave me up for adoption meant that she would have to share negative memories of a son whom she had already lost. John was dead, and with that, all the negative memories were rarely spoken of. Mom and Dad were rebuilding their life without John and burying painful memories and heartache. I couldn't hurt them by rehashing the past.

My birth mom, Karen, would have been considered an acquaintance at best. We barely spoke, and when we did, it was a casual, stilted conversation that revolved around niceties. I wasn't comfortable asking her why she decided on or agreed to my adoption. I didn't feel as if I had the right to ask her such personal questions about her past. Now I wonder if I was putting everyone else's feelings before mine or if I was too afraid to ask the difficult questions. The answers may have hurt more than the unknown.

I was so fortunate to have a family that not only accepted me but loved me as one of their own. My parents, William, Nicole, my aunts, and cousins were constants in my life. We shared holidays, birthdays, graduations, and weddings together.

How could I selfishly want more? They gave me the gift of undying love and devotion, the type that every child longs for. It was freely given to me by my parents. I received far more than I ever lost.

I thought I had come to terms with not knowing the details of why I was adopted. I told myself that it wouldn't change the circumstances of my life. If anything, it would just open old memories that my family had worked hard to forget.

I didn't realize that even though I wasn't talking about my feelings, they were still festering and growing, nagging at me during the worst possible times. During times that I should have been happy or enjoying life, self-doubt and jealousy would creep back in and steal my joy. It was a painful cycle that followed me into adulthood.

I no longer wished for my life to be different, only for answers and closure. Given the choice, I would not have left my parents for another life.

The material things are of little consequence to me now—instead, it is the love and affection that I received from them that matters. Being the only child still at home had a lot of advantages: more free time, extra money, and attention to what truly mattered.

There was not a day that went by that I didn't feel loved. I was adopted as a newborn, so my grandparents have always and will always be my parents. Seeing family and sacrifice through their eyes gives me a different perspective of family and devotion. Not everyone is wired to step up and love a child as their own. They had raised both of their sons. It was time for them to rest and be grandparents, but instead they became parents again to a newborn.

They went through all the midnight feedings, sickness, teething, dating, and teenage years with me. I was never an inconvenience to them. They taught me what it was like to love someone more than you did yourself. They put me first before anything else in their world. I didn't have to compete for attention or love. I am blessed because they chose to raise me. I am blessed because my birth parents put their pain aside to do what was best for me.

Since Mom was a stay-at-home mom, I had her undivided attention most days. We played endless hours of Barbies and baby dolls. She watched more episodes of *She-Ra* with me than I am sure she cared to remember. I ate in front of the TV, leaving crumbs and stains on her white doilies, without being scolded. Keeping the house spotless didn't take precedence over me. If given the choice to clean or do something with me, she chose me. I was never lectured about my toys being thrown all over the house. She didn't force me to clean them up after playtime. Instead, they lay in the same spot until I sat down to play again.

When I was a young child, Mom enrolled me at Nan's Academy where I took weekly classes in ballet, tap, and baton. These classes required time and funds for monthly dues, practice clothing, and recital outfits. None of that was of concern to Mom. I don't know if the fees for attending classes hurt us financially, because she never mentioned it. She didn't complain about taking me to practice weekly or sitting in the waiting room while I lived my best life.

Mom bought every picture package available for my recitals and cheered the loudest for me from the audience. She wasn't mistaken about my capabilities—she knew that these classes were only for fun. When I had my fill of them, she didn't push me to go back and continue dancing. Instead, she allowed me to move on to my next interest. What I remember most about those activities was Mom's devotion to me. She was always there, even when she didn't feel like it. She was one of the first parents to volunteer to help with fundraisers or events because she wanted to help the program grow.

Dad worked daily, no matter the job, to provide for us. During layoffs from the mines, he worked as a janitor at the high school. He took his responsibility seriously and didn't ever shy away from it. As a coal miner, he was usually gone more than he was home, and he gladly accepted any overtime offered. With an unmatched work ethic, he went to work sick or in bad weather. His dedication to providing for us was so important that he worked until the day before he had a heart catheterization. The test showed major blockages that required an emergency triple bypass surgery.

I think of his willpower and ability to push through any obstacle. I was always proud of Dad because of how hard he worked and how he valued our family. I saw him as a man who would go to any lengths to protect us.

After his surgery, Dad was forced to retire. With his demanding job no longer taking him away 40-plus hours a week, we spent more time together. He would take me out for bike rides in the high school parking lot or sit on the porch and watch me swing for hours. It didn't matter what we did together; it was just being with him that I loved. I was Daddy's doll, the person who made his eyes light up and a smile spread across his face.

I now understand why Mom and Dad attempted to shelter me so much when I was growing up. They only wanted me to have a childhood of happiness and security. I can recall true joy and love while at the same time remembering pain and anger. I think that's part of life, what each of us experience. During heartache and sadness, we must hang on to what is truly important.

Throughout the years I have formed my own opinions about my adoption, based on a mixture of memories, assumptions, and rumors. I don't have all the answers, and I never will. That's okay now because I know the important, high-level reasoning for my adoption. Not being in the weeds of the details protects my memories of everyone.

I believe sacrifice and love have a direct correlation to one another. When you love someone, you value their happiness far more than your own. You put their needs and wants above others. I love my family—my husband and my children. I would do anything for them even if it hurt me, except the one choice that my birth parents made. They made the most unselfish decision of anyone I know: allowing my paternal grandparents to adopt me.

I can't imagine how hard that decision must have been. As a mother, I can't fathom allowing someone else to raise my child as I watch from afar. My birth parents loved me enough to do it. They loved me enough to walk away and give me a wonderful life with two parents who loved me and made me their entire world.

CHAPTER 26

The Gift

*She put me first, above how she felt, above
what was going on in her life.*

Making peace with all the unknown answers about my birth mom and her side of the family hasn't been easy. My lack of family knowledge has been made painfully aware to me in unexpected situations, such as providing my family medical history at the doctor's office. Karen's side is always blank. In those moments, I am forced to share that I was adopted and have no knowledge of her medical history, except for lung cancer. Not knowing my medical history is more technical than emotional.

The emotional side of the unawareness was visibly present when I realized that I didn't know her parents, my maternal grandparents. I have no recollection of her mom or when she passed. As an adult, I attended my maternal grandfather's funeral, without ever knowing him. To my knowledge, we never spoke or saw each other. If so, it was in passing, and I had no idea who he was. I'm not sure if he knew who I was. We lived in a very small town but seemed to avoid each other, either by accident or intent.

I don't know if Karen grew up close to her parents, if she was the oldest in her family, or how many siblings she had. I know very little about her family structure or whether she was the silly, dramatic, or withdrawn sibling. There are no stories to recall about family traditions on her side. I can't share a single story with my children about her childhood.

That is a heartache that is hard to explain. For a long while, I viewed myself as half of a human, unknown to the other half of myself. I was curious if my laugh was more like Karen's than John's. What about my mannerisms? Did I have similar interests as my other siblings? Question after question built in my mind for years, without any definitive answers.

I don't have a wealth of memories that I can recount of my time with Karen or old pictures to jog my memory. Instead, I am left with brief encounters and glimpses into her life. As a daughter, I wish I had more to share, not for this book but just for myself and my kids. I am passing down a vacancy to my children that they will never be able to fill.

At the fault of no one, Karen's life is a mystery to me. I can speculate and piece stories together that I have heard, but little comes from true experience. The small pieces of information divulged to me over the years are barely enough to construct a family tree or an account of Karen's life.

I spent years trading niceties with family members instead of forming a bond. This bond wasn't hindered because of restrictions or laws; it just didn't happen. My mom told me about my adoption before I was old enough to grasp what it meant, so there was no hiding the truth from me. I grew up knowing I was adopted and who my birth mother was. I just didn't really know her.

My parents did not forbid Karen to visit me or have a relationship with me—they encouraged it. To them, Karen was still family and was welcome at their home anytime. She chose to watch me grow up from afar so that my life wasn't interrupted or more complicated.

Repeatedly, I was told by both of my parents that she was a good person. As a kid that was all I needed to know. Mom believed in her, so why shouldn't I? They loved Karen and were indebted to her for allowing them to raise me.

For most of my childhood, Karen and I lived within five minutes of each other. Living so close to one another, we still managed to keep a distance that was never fully bridged. We drove past her and other family members regularly, with usually only a wave. On occasion we would stop and speak, but it was always short and insignificant. Or was it? Were those small conversations laying the groundwork for me to reach out one day? A simple wave and "How are you?" were the building blocks to what may have been.

Recalling the times she was around while I was growing up, I was nervous, not afraid of her. More so, I was afraid that I would say or do something wrong. I was overly cautious about what I said, analyzing every comment before it was spoken. My eyes wandered through the entire room without landing on her face. I could not look at her directly—instead, I focused on anything else in the room. If we ever hugged, I don't remember it. There was an invisible divide between us that we both respected.

I wonder if my apprehension and uneasiness are what kept her away. Did I make her feel uncomfortable or unwanted? Or was it too painful to see me? I will never know for sure. I hope that she understood why I was reserved or standoffish. I was never angry at her for not keeping me, only confused and grateful. Being confused and grateful at the same time are two very different emotions to reconcile. The life she gave me was filled with love and support that I wouldn't trade for anything in this world. I only wish she would have been a bigger part of it.

Now, I have a better understanding of how she put me first. Every Christmas she sent me a present by way of my siblings. The gift tag always read, "To Brandi Dawn, From [blank]." I grew up expecting those visits every Christmas. It was not the gift that was delivered that I cared about; it was the company. Starting the day before Christmas Eve, I would pace to and from the living room side window, watching for David, my older brother by Karen, to walk around the bottom road. Sometimes my younger brother and sister came with him; other times it was my older cousin. Back then I saw them as living their best lives. They were wild, happy, and free. They basically came and went as they pleased, free to have fun and roam, whereas I was kept close to home and watched.

I looked up to David and my older cousins and wanted to be more like them—self-assured, strong, and fearless. Instead, I feared everything. I was afraid to speak up and be myself, afraid to ask for what I really wanted, and afraid to put myself out in the front of life.

Our visit always started in the living room with Mom and Dad talking with David and whoever else was with him. While in front of Mom and Dad, David always tried to wrangle everyone else and function as if he were the responsible one, telling the others to quieten down even though he was the loudest of all of them visiting. He acted as if he oversaw everything, even when no one was listening.

After we exchanged gifts in the living room, Mom always coaxed us into the kitchen with sweet treats. The counters and table were usually covered with homemade fudge, fruits, cakes, and other sweets. David's favorite, also my favorite, was the two-toned peanut butter–chocolate fudge. Mom always seemed to have extra hidden that was meant for him to take home. She loved David, and her way of showing it was with food. I believe he knew that, because he always made a point to gush over everything she fixed.

Reflecting on those Christmas gifts, I realize that was Karen always acknowledging me, saying, "I haven't forgotten you. You will always be in my heart, even if not in my life." I can't imagine how it must have felt for her to shop for a child she wasn't raising, to send a gift by her son instead of bringing it herself. I have wondered why she didn't come herself. I now have come to believe there are several reasons why she didn't bring the gifts herself: it was too painful for her, or she didn't want to confuse me or dampen the holiday spirit.

She put me first, above how she felt, above what was going on in her life. She did what she thought was best for me. Isn't that what a true mother does—put the best interest of their kids first? I wish my young heart could have realized all of that then.

She may not have been in my immediate circle, but she was in the background watching. It was years later that I was made aware of all the times she attended my school events and stayed in the shadows. During most of my homecoming court ceremonies, she watched from the sidelines, never approaching me or letting me know she was there. I wonder how she felt during those moments. Was she sad, happy, or proud? Maybe a mixture of all three?

Mom and Karen would talk on the phone sometimes for hours. Mom giving her a full recap of my life, from grades to friends, to current interests. She was learning about her daughter from someone else. She didn't walk away, even though I didn't see that as a child. She stayed in contact with Mom, always a phone call away. That's respectful and loving.

CHAPTER 27
A New Relationship

We didn't discuss the past or why decisions were made;
instead, we just picked up where we were.

Knowing my birth mother as an adult allowed me to see a different side of her. When I was a child, she was this aloof person whom I wasn't sure if I should fear, be angry at, or love. Depending on when you talked to me, you may have received one or two of those responses in a singular conversation. I knew who she was physically but not emotionally or mentally.

The relationship that she and my parents shared was one of respect and love. As an adult and mother, I can imagine it was difficult to maintain that type of relationship on both sides. The way she treated my parents told me all I needed to know about her. She was friendly and loving toward Mom and Dad. She truly went out of her way to protect Mom a few times. Mom never hid the fact that she loved Karen and that she was grateful to her for allowing them to adopt me. If anything, Mom told me frequently how grateful she was to Karen.

Once the decision was made, Karen did not interfere with my childhood. She didn't try to confuse me or make me feel uncomfortable—instead she kept her distance from me and only approached me if my parents or I invited it. She put my well-being above herself. Her ability to walk away from me is one of the reasons I love her. She demonstrated unselfishness in a way I don't think I could have. My adoption didn't sever the relationship between Mom and Karen. In fact, it made it stronger and more permanent.

In 2006 Karen was in jail. I never asked what the charges were for, and I have no desire to know now. While Karen was in jail, my mom was diagnosed with lung cancer, and the prognosis wasn't good. It was unlikely that she would be alive when Karen was released. Before it was too late, Mom wanted to have one more conversation with the young girl whom she had cared for and watched grow up. So, my older brother, David— Karen's son—arranged the phone call. No one knows what was said between the two of them, but I know it brought peace to Mom. After they hung up, Mom sat in her burgundy chair and cried tears of relief.

Karen had turned her life over to God, and Mom couldn't have been happier. She told me that evening that Karen was going to be okay, that she was finally the person that she was meant to be. She didn't live to see Karen get out of jail, but at least they were able to talk one more time.

Karen was released from jail shortly after Mom's funeral. She didn't attempt to contact me or let me know she had been released. I don't remember who told me she had been released from prison, maybe Dad or David. I thought about calling or visiting her after I found out but decided against it. I didn't really know what to say or how to approach her after not seeing her for so many years. Instead, I called David to check on him and her. He was the person who kept me connected to the rest of the family.

I finally worked up my courage to call her a few months after I talked with David. Part of me was hoping that she wouldn't answer the phone, because I didn't know what to say. I didn't know if I should apologize for not writing or visiting while she was in jail or act as if no time had lapsed.

We didn't form a mother-daughter bond, but it was more than friendship. I would almost label it as a protective relationship. I had this sense of safety because of her. I don't know if that was because I viewed her as someone strong willed and tough or because of an underlying bond that I didn't know was there.

I felt that Karen had more to say to me but wasn't prepared to share it with me yet. Her guard was up, I assume, to protect both of us from reliving the past. At the time I didn't contain the bandwidth to ask questions about her childhood or the circumstances that led up to my adoption. Processing Mom's death and the birth of my son was more than my fragile heart and mind could handle.

We spoke sporadically after Braden was born, but we didn't visit one another. I didn't have the space in my life for anyone else. My heart was so vulnerable that I feared allowing anyone else to become close to me. So, I kept everyone at arm's length as a protective mechanism. She didn't insert herself into my life; in fact, she rarely called me. If we spoke, I usually initiated the conversation.

About three years later, Dad was unexpectedly diagnosed with terminal lung cancer, with the only option being palliative radiation therapy. From the day of his diagnosis, he lived less than a month. I couldn't believe that I was facing another death so soon. I acted as if I were holding it together on the outside, while on the inside I was destroyed. I was so angry and hurt that I was ready to lash out at anyone, which I did on more than one occasion. It didn't take me long to realize that I had a temper like both of my birth parents.

I was no longer this sad person whom you felt sorry for. I was angry and snapped at anyone who stepped out of line. I was always negative and ready for a fight with the person closest to me, who was my then boyfriend, Jamie. Everyone else just saw a closed-off version of who I was.

At Dad's funeral a person came in whom I had very hard feelings against, and that's being nice. To share what was truly in my heart would be too graphic. I blamed them for the years of pain that my parents and John went through. I believed they were the reason I lost John and that my parents' lives were no more than a shell. So, to see that person at my dad's funeral was too much for me. I stood up, prepared to make a fool out of myself, when Karen caught my eye. Until I stood up, I didn't even know she was there.

She was shaking her head angrily at me with a look that could have cut me open. David was standing beside her, also shaking his head while smiling. Well, I ignored her gesture and started toward the person when she cut me off.

"Brandi Dawn, you will not make a scene at this funeral," she said, pushing me into the hallway area out of view from the other guests. "This is not the time or place to do or say anything."

By that point, I was adding shock to my emotions because she had never spoken to me in a stern voice, and I don't say that lightly. I could tell by the look on her face that I was making a bad decision. So, I didn't act on my impulse out loud, only in my mind. She was right—my dad would have been devastated had I caused a scene. Taking the high road wasn't always easy, but it was the right thing to do. Had she not been there, it's no telling what I would have said or done that evening in the funeral home. That was the first time that she acted like a parent and interfered with anything that I wanted to do. I am glad she was there and stopped me from making a fool out of myself and an embarrassment of Dad's funeral.

I thought after that episode that maybe we could have a stronger relationship. I had no idea that less than a month later she would also be diagnosed with lung cancer. Damn it! Cancer, specifically lung cancer, was hitting our family harder than I could handle. I was angry and confused, with no idea of where I stood in this horrific situation. I wasn't a daughter who had been raised by her. So many of her family members deserved time with her and a say over her treatment. I didn't have a right. I wanted to be there for her and the rest of my siblings, but I was an impostor. There were aunts, uncles, and cousins showing up whom I didn't know. I was in a new world without a guide.

During one of our conversations, I realized that Karen had always been there for me even when I didn't notice. She had pictures from all my recitals, cheerleading years, and homecoming courts. She stood in the shadows and watched as I was living my life. All those times I thought she didn't care, but it was the opposite. She did care. She cared more than I knew.

We didn't discuss the past or why decisions were made; instead, we just picked up where we were. In a months' time, we both grew to know one another in the present, while leaving the past where it belonged. Near New Year's, Karen took her final breath, and with it went my past. I went from four parents to none. In my early 30s, I was parentless. It was a new world for me to navigate.

My view of her may differ from others'. I admire and respect her. She gave me a gift that wasn't easy, a gift that no mother can give without hurting herself. She gave me my parents. She gave me a life that consisted of a stable home and loving family. For that, I will always be grateful. I will always see the selfless side of Karen, before all else.

I am speaking in assumptions, but I believe she loved my birth father, my parents, and me—not only loved all of us but respected us. You can love someone and still make decisions that are not best for them, but she put us first. Her decisions were always what was best for me, not herself. She stayed close to Mom and Dad even though they were raising her little girl. She showed them respect by not interfering or overstepping any lines.

I am grateful for our time together and my ability to have peace and understanding over my adoption. I fully recognize that so many others are not as lucky as I am. I had four parents whom I knew and who loved me. In the end, that is most important.

CHAPTER 28
Bonding

He cried. I cried. We both told each other that we loved each other.

Family are those people who choose to be in your life and love you, blood or not! An uncle may be more of a dad than your own father. A cousin may feel more like a sister than your blood siblings. That's okay. They are your people! As a child I privately obsessed about the family members who were not in my life, the family who I knew by name only. I was bitter that my other siblings had one another to grow up with. I was bitter that my birth parents didn't want to raise me.

I wasn't raised with my older brother David, but that didn't stop him from portraying the older brother when it suited him. With a larger-than-life personality and temper that could make people tremble, he was a force to be dealt with. I didn't tell him, but I was so proud to be his little sister. He wasn't intimidated by anything. The boy would stand up to the biggest guy in the school, or a grown man for that matter.

He tried to stay in my life from the time we were kids. He would pop through the door for a visit with his mouth already running before the door was even open. That's how my dad always described him.

"Well, hello, old man," David would say to Dad.

Dad would always chuckle and say, "Well, hello, young man."

David would walk over and plop down on the couch beside me. "Well, what do you say?"

"Not much. What about you?" Dad would ask.

"Well, you know me. I am always into something." Looking over at me, he'd ask, "Well, what do you say, young lady?"

I always rolled my eyes at him and laughed because I had no idea how to respond.

Sometimes our cousin Scott would come with him. Scott towered over David in height but was the quieter of the two. Scott was a talented artist, so much so that he drew quilt patterns for Mom to cut out. They weren't blood family to my parents, but both of my parents loved them and always welcomed them into our family.

One of my favorite memories of our time together was playing Mario on the Nintendo in Mom's sitting room. Conveniently, the sitting room was attached to the kitchen, which made it easy to grab snacks from the counter. David and Scott were rather good at Mario—me not so much. I was too focused on collecting every coin than making it to the next level quickly. It drove them crazy watching me run back to grab a coin I missed. They would always remind me of the time clock and urge me to run faster, which caused me to go slower a few times just to annoy them.

David loved to give everyone a hard time, and Scott would quickly jump on board to help. I was so gullible when I was young that I was a perfect target. I believed whatever they said. So, he took full advantage of my naivete during one of his visits. I was eating a microwave French bread pizza, the small rectangle pizzas with the rounded edge and small triangle pepperonis. It was my favorite lunch back then, especially the round side. I know that's crazy, but I always thought it tasted better. As I was eating, he told me that pepperoni was made of goat meat.

Ugh! No way, I thought.

He assured me it was a fact. His laugh echoed through the house as he watched me pick each one of them off my pizza. Still to this day, even though I have been told a million times and I know the truth myself, I still pick off the pepperoni over 50% of the time. Thanks, David!

David, as the oldest brother on my birth mom's side, was the dominant one of that family. The other siblings did as he said without question.

Heck, I did what he said, and I didn't live with him. He was the guy who didn't just run his mouth, which he did a lot. He was also the guy who would back it up. He was cocky and a total ladies' man in high school. I can recall several arguments that resulted in fights over him. Some of the girls had this crazy jealous hatred for each other that lasted into adulthood. The upside to being his sister is all the girls were nice to me. Maybe they thought I could influence him. Anyone who knew David knew that wasn't possible. He made up his own mind without consulting others.

I remember sitting in the classroom one day and hearing someone say, "Hey that's David fighting Keith." I hate to admit it, but I was proud and nervous at the same time. I was proud of him for being so brave but nervous that he would get hurt. I stayed away from the window; the play-by-play account by others was enough for me. I don't remember who won the fight, so I would call it a draw.

During my junior year of high school, I was crazy over this older guy who had just graduated from high school. Crazy is probably an understatement—he was the main focus of my life. I literally waited by the phone for him to call. Mom and Dad had always been strict about whom I was allowed to date, and car dates were practically not allowed. So, it was already hard for me to see my new obsession. With him being older than I was and free to come and go as he pleased; I was at a disadvantage with him.

After begging and fighting with my parents to allow him to come to our house one evening, they finally gave in. I don't think I had ever been so nervous in my life. I paced the floor waiting for him to pop up over the steps, and when he did, I smiled so big that I am certain the corners of my mouth touched my ears. When Dad saw my reaction, his eyes got small and his stare at Jacob was intense. Either Jacob didn't notice, or he was cocky enough to not care.

Either way, Dad went on to bed as he always did and left Mom to supervise us. That night I got up my courage to ask Jacob to go to my junior prom with me. When he said yes, I felt as if I had won the lottery. My heart was beating so fast that I am sure you could see it through my shirt.

The next morning Dad held no words back in letting me know what he thought of Jacob. "What man wears an earbob? He even had a damn necklace on—is he a girl?"

I tried to defend Jacob because I loved his earring and necklace. Heck, I liked everything about him.

Dad said, "He came up on the porch strutting like he owned the house. You don't need to see him."

Tears started flowing, and my begging changed to anger the longer we talked about it. Once Dad had made up his mind only Mom was going to change it. So, I retreated and waited to talk with Mom later.

I don't know how David knew that Jacob had come to our house the night before or that I had asked him to prom, but he found out. David came through our front door with an arsenal full of complaints and stories about Jacob. With no uncertain terms, he did not want me to see Jacob. Dad was already against the idea, and when David shared his stories, my fate was sealed.

David sat there all smug on the couch because he knew he had won that argument. I was so mad at him that I swore I would never speak to him again. He had no right to interfere in my life or with whom I dated. I knew the reason he didn't like Jacob was over another girl. It had nothing to do with who Jacob really was.

Fast-forward to the current day, and Dad and David were both right! When I say I dodged a bullet, I mean I dodged a bomb. Jacob had made several bad decisions that ultimately resulted in severe legal problems. David was always there for me even when I didn't realize it. He took care of things in the background and stood up for me when I was being picked on.

David had always maintained a close relationship with Mom and Dad, even when I wasn't there. It was understandable that after Mom was diagnosed with lung cancer, David would want to visit her more often. She fought so hard to beat cancer, but it was evident to those who were able to accept it that she would lose her battle. David's presence helped improve Mom's mood. He had a way of making her laugh even when she didn't feel well.

I know that David was hurt over Mom's passing, but he put my well-being before his own. David knew how close Mom and I were. At the funeral he could tell that I was at my breaking point, that saying good-bye to "my person" was too much. He also saw how Dad was affected. A strong, stoic man was brought down to his knees.

The evening after the funeral, Dad and I were at the house by our-selves. With Dad in his recliner and me on the couch recliner, we sat in complete quietness. The only sound was Dad inhaling and exhaling the smoke from his cigarette, until the doorbell rang. Eager for a distraction, Dad and I both went to the door. Seeing David behind the storm door was a relief; the house instantly felt less empty and dark.

He walked in with a cigarette in his hand, saying his usual greeting, "What do you say, old man?"

I was relieved that we had company at the house, especially him. He kept the conversation upbeat and ongoing till later that night.

He stood up with the same haste he entered with, saying, "Well, y'all better get your beauty sleep. You need it." His showing up that night was a godsend to me and Dad. He was exactly who we needed.

After that night we started having regular phone conversations. He was so entertaining to talk to. You know the people who animate their conversations to a degree that you belly laugh—that was him every time we talked. He talked about his kids with such pride and fear. His three daughters were gorgeous and totally independent; they took "having your hands full" to an entirely new level. They were a combo of both of their parents. I couldn't help but snicker, thinking he had finally met his match. His kids were his reason for everything he did. He loved every minute of it. It was odd to see him transform from the wild ladies' man to the stern dad, but he handled both positions well.

During my last pregnancy, I had some complications, and David was ready to help by sending someone to stay with me or by coming to the hospital himself. Most importantly, he showed he cared. Those phone calls allowed us to be more like brother and sister than ever before. He cried. I cried. We both told each other that we loved each other. I meant it. I know that he did too.

Little did I know that a year later he would die suddenly. I was shaken with guilt and what ifs. My heart broke for his kids, for his girlfriend, and for all his family. He was one of the strongest and most loving men that I have ever known. Now make no mistake, he stood his ground when need be and told others exactly what he thought. He did it because he cared. He did it because he wanted everyone else whom he loved to do better—to be better. He served as a protector to so many family members. He was the person who always helped you, even if you were wrong.

The family was so kind to me. I had aunts and cousins who barely knew me, but they welcomed me. I am so grateful that I was able to say goodbye to my brother and hug my nieces. His kids are so self-sufficient and loving. They have been through so much at a young age, but it's not stopped them. I am in awe of them.

Now I see that I wasn't excluded from their family because they didn't love me. It was quite the opposite. My birth mother gave me up because she loved me. She gave me a better life. That family—my family—has always included me anytime I included myself. It's not always easy to include yourself. I still struggle with stepping into my nieces' lives. I don't feel as if I have the right to intrude now after being gone for so long. At the same time, I want to be a part of their lives and watch their kids grow up.

It's hard to reach out to someone when you haven't always been there, when you missed the big moments of their lives. How do you just walk in the front door and say, "Now I want to be here for you"? I wish I had the magic answer for that, but I don't. Instead, I decided to start trying to be more present in their lives, even if it was over text.

I no longer feel uncomfortable reaching out to them—I know that it will take time to forge a bond like I hope we will have one day. For now, I am grateful to share in their lives, both the happy and sad. I listen to them when they need someone to talk with, but I am careful about not providing too much advice. They are strong young women now, who can—and do—think for themselves.

CHAPTER 29
Help

The difference between him and me is I finally did ask for help.

Accepting your faults is not easy. Changing them is even harder. Had John asked for help as a young child, this story may not have been written. He may have gotten his dyslexia under control and learned how to read and write without embarrassment. Later in life when he was placed in and out of rehab and jail, he could have used that time to get sober, to detox, and to let go of his demons. Instead, he chose not to accept the help he needed.

As I reexamined each of my family members, I realized that we had similar negative traits and that how we managed those determined the quality of life that we had. John and I both tried to conceal our faults instead of accepting and learning from them. John's inability to ask for or accept help with his reading changed his life and our entire family. My inability to admit that I was depressed and struggling with low self-worth caused me to not build the life I was dreaming of.

The difference between him and me is I finally did ask for help. I looked in my son's eyes and knew that no matter what I didn't want him to grow up feeling the way I did. I wanted him to have a parent who was whole and present, instead of fake and exhausted. I wanted a better life for myself, something that I could be truly proud of. I wanted to be a person whom others respected because I did the right things.

I realized to be the person I wanted to be, I had to change the person

I was. My first step at changing my life was attending counseling. When I first started going, I was humiliated that I needed help and was adamant that no one could know. The visits were exhausting. I would leave and feel as if I had no energy left, that my only option was to sleep. The first visit was primarily intake, she asked me a lot of open-ended questions and listened contently as I rambled. I left that visit feeling guilty for telling her about John's suicide. It felt like a betrayal.

So, the next visit I was mentally prepared to keep my walls up and not allow myself to share further negative info about my family. I don't know how she did it, but she broke me down again. There I sat, telling her things that I had not told anyone. I thought, What the hell? How is she able to draw out these insecurities and hurt feelings that I had buried so deep that I didn't even know they still existed?

Over the next several days, I felt guilty once again. I had betrayed my family by telling her things that shouldn't have been shared. "Ugh! Why was I allowing someone to judge my family?" I said out loud while driving home after work one evening, "Forget it, I'm not going back. All this is doing is bringing up things that are better off forgotten." That was that; I had tried counseling, and it wasn't for me. I was not going to allow myself to talk negatively about my family or focus on the past.

Well, as the next week drug on, I kept putting off calling to cancel. I didn't have the time, or I didn't feel up to it. Blah, blah! I waited until the day before the appointment and decided it was too rude to cancel at such short notice. So, the next morning I made the one-hour drive to Abingdon. Yes, the one-hour drive—I couldn't allow myself to go to counseling close to home in fear that someone may find out.

I realized that as a child I buried so deeply the anger I felt toward John that I didn't recognize it until years later. I had been so focused on being there for Mom that I didn't address what his decisions did to me. Anger broke me in a way that I will never be healed. Instead, I am a repaired vase with glue holding my heart together.

I didn't understand depression or grief. I didn't realize the toll that it would take on your body both mentally and physically. Looking back, I understand why that little girl sat there with emptiness in her heart and soul. She wasn't grieving only for herself but for her parents as well. Her life was never the same again. She carried her grief with theirs. She was thrust into a scary, dark adult world that she couldn't comprehend.

John's addiction changed our family forever. My mom and dad drifted further apart. Mom believed that Dad was too hard on John and not supportive, and Dad believed Mom was too soft. I don't know who was right or wrong, but I see both sides. They were both fighting for the life of their child, for their entire family. They were both mentally and physically exhausted.

Dad was a man of few words when it came to discussing his feelings or emotions. I'm confident that he was devastated over losing John, but he kept it inside. I cannot recall a single conversation that Dad and I had about John's alcoholism or suicide. From an outside perspective, it may have appeared that Dad was unaffected by John's death, but that wasn't the case. Dad filled his time with work, gardening, yard work, housework, and other tasks to keep his mind from thinking of the past. He wasn't a man who sat idle. If he was awake, he wanted to be doing something productive. I assume staying busy is how Dad coped with his sadness.

I have wondered for years if he ever had anyone whom he was able to talk with about John's suicide. I know that he and Mom saw John differently. I don't think either of them was able to give the other any comfort or understanding. They both had misgivings about how the other treated John—there was nothing that was going to bridge that gap. At some point they stopped discussing John. It was easier for their relationship to heal by not speaking of the elephant in the room.

Mom grieved in waves that not everyone truly saw or understood. There were days, maybe weeks at a time, that she was grouchy with or easily perturbed by other people. She seemed distant and not engaged in certain situations or with certain people. But those actions or inactions were only a defense mechanism to protect herself from more pain. Losing

John the way she did altered her spirit to such a level that she was never whole again. You cannot understand the pain she felt unless you were there in those minutes of the gun being fired and his body rolled out.

The screams that came from her could only be the sounds of someone destroyed. Watching her in those shocking moments made me hurt for her more than I ever did for myself. To a certain level, she lived vicariously through her children. Her personal value was based on how we performed.

Mom and I were closer than most could understand. We confided in each other about everything. She knew far more about me than she wanted to know. She was my best friend, and I was hers. If I had a choice of spending time with her or friends, I often chose her. She was someone who was there for me no matter how she felt. I always knew that she loved me and put me first. I know she had nothing left to give after John's death, but she pushed herself for me.

Even after I became an adult, it was difficult for Mom to talk about John. Acknowledging his actions meant reliving them and feeling that same sadness and helplessness that she felt when they occurred. Our conversations always ended in her crying and sounding removed. Mom's voice would become more robotic until she wasn't the one talking. Her heart and mind had checked out of the conversation. She needed me to see the good John, the one whom she saw. I wanted to see that John too. I wanted to only remember the good times, but the bad times were real, and they were a part of me, either because I lived them or because I heard the stories.

I spent years struggling with John's suicide. I kept making it about me and how it changed my life, how it changed my parents' life, and how we were never the same again. My mom never let go of the pain. She was changed forever. She existed in a constant state of sadness and pretend happiness. Our pain was horrible. My pain is still hard to bear, but I can't imagine how John must have felt that morning.

My sadness and loneliness cannot compare to what he must have been feeling. He was lost and scared and couldn't see his way to a better place.

Years of guilt and embarrassment were lodged in his heart and brain. He felt useless and reckless with those whom he loved the most. He believed that the world would be better off without him.

I can't imagine feeling as if the world would be better off without me. I can't fathom what it felt like to know that you had hurt everyone you love over and over and that you couldn't stop. He didn't kill himself because he was selfish; he did it because he wanted the pain to stop for all of us.

I believe that John was humiliated over his addiction and felt genuine remorse for his actions. He didn't want to be the person depending on alcohol and hurting others in his path. I must believe that he wanted to change, but he didn't have the professional help needed. Dyslexia, the underlying issue for his drinking, needed to be addressed first. Once a plan for the stimulus was implemented, he could have worked through his issues of low self-esteem, anger, etc. It wouldn't have been easy or fast. It would have taken a lot of work and understanding to get through all the years and barrage of feelings within our family. Our family could have and would have done it with him; of this, I am sure.

I am certain there were times that he genuinely tried to stop drinking, but the thought of leaving the comfort of the known for the unknown won every time. He understood how to operate in the world of alcohol. He knew it would numb the pain and provide an outlet to not face his feelings. While drinking, he was not responsible for his actions; it was always the alcohol's fault. That singular statement gave him complete deniability of his actions, or so he thought.

As a child, I suffered at the hands of others who didn't understand the situation I was in. There were times I was made fun of and shunned. Some kids thought they were better than me and let me know it. I was told, "I am not allowed to play with you. I have heard some moms say you come from a bad family." On the contrary, I did not come from a bad family. I come from a wonderful family that showed me how to be a good person, how to love others, and how to always be kind. I was raised with a work ethic and a hard line of right and wrong.

Judgmental treatment occurs far too often and to far too many people who let it go unresolved. Too many children are judged harshly for something they have no control over. When children hear their parents say negative comments about a child and their family, that child will repeat it. It is a circle of pain and harshness that needs to stop in this world. We as adults should show our children how to treat others. I am fortunate that, for every rude adult or kid, I had someone positive in my corner.

I share all of this for the kids who are not as fortunate as I was and am. Think of the ones who need support and guidance—the ones who do not have a safe home or good parents to be with. I had those things, and that's why I will be a voice for the kids who do not.

Children who come from a bad home life or have experienced trauma need support and encouragement. Instead of judging them, include them. Show them possibilities instead of limiting them.

It doesn't matter what a family member may or may not have done. Don't speak negatively about the child or exclude them from your kid's life. Instead, support that child and give them the belief they can do anything. They may break the generational curse because of your support.

Show a little grace to the person you are talking about. Is it information that needs to be shared with others? If not, don't say it. How can that person ever get the opportunity to change when they are constantly beaten down?

What you say to a child or about a child will stick with them forever. Even after they grow up and see their true value, those cruel words will always be in the back of their mind. At the time, I was weak and not able to stand up for myself or my parents. Now I would say, "Screw you. I don't want to play with you." I would love to rewind time and say, "Yes, John was sometimes reckless and dangerous—he was also scared and sick. When sober, he was kind and funny. You cannot lump him into a specific set of negative characteristics because that is unjust to who he was. His negative actions were not a reflection of my parents or me."

I'm not just saying that my parents were good people. They demonstrated it by the way they lived their lives. They didn't drink. They didn't take drugs. They worked hard. They volunteered in the community. They helped others in need. They didn't deserve that type of treatment or rude comments. When John was sober, he was a lot like them, giving, helpful, and thoughtful.

I will never be okay with others judging kids for something they had no control over. It's absurd to think that adults would instill hurtful habits into their own children. When a parent or any adult makes derogatory comments about other children in front of children, they participate in bully behavior. Think before you speak. When I was a child, those instances hurt, but they did not break me. If anything, I believe I am better because of what happened to me as a child.

I was fortunate that for every rude comment or shunned behavior I had people who showed true kindness and compassion. They didn't judge me over my birth father. They accepted me for who I was, for the person whom I was growing up to be.

My childhood made me more compassionate and understanding. I always try to see the good in others even when they are hiding it. I understand that someone with a substance use disorder is not a bad person. They are making poor choices. I do not group the two together. I do not and will not pardon an addict's behavior, but I will be the first to support them when they are ready to fight the disease.

I miss John and wonder what our lives would have been like if he were still alive. I wonder if Mom would have still been happy or if the worry would have broken her the same way. I think about Dad and his health issues and wonder if the stress and pain he kept on the inside caused him to be physically sick. I look in the mirror at myself and wonder if I would have been so broken if John had not committed suicide.

I will never know those answers for sure. What I do know is that he is no longer in pain. He is no longer fighting an inner demon that I will never understand. I know that my parents loved and hurt deeply. I know that I can heal my heart from an unimaginable pain. I know that I may break, but I can be rebuilt stronger.

CHAPTER 30

Healing

When I was finally in a place where I could fully appreciate the positive people and experiences I've encountered, my mindset started to change.

You are not your past! You are not your family! You are not your mistakes! You are you, the person who is reading this book and the person who can decide to be anyone they want to be! You can decide to change your life's trajectory at any time. There is nothing in this world holding you back but you. Your life doesn't need to be dominated by past failures. I know that can be easier said than done when you are struggling with your own demons. It's hard to make a fresh start and feel as if you can conquer the world—but you can!

I'm not asking you to take a leap of grave proportion. I am asking you to take a step in a new direction, a direction that is lit by opportunities, new adventures, and possibilities. Look in your heart of hearts and allow yourself to dream. If you were uninhibited by your past, what would you dream of becoming or doing? We all have dreams even when we feel as if they are unreachable. We just don't allow them to take root. That's the dream that I hope you transform into a goal.

For years I allowed depression and low self-worth to control my life. I was the champion for poor, pitiful me. I had an awful childhood. I used the traumatic events in my childhood as a crutch instead of a springboard. Hiding behind my pain allowed me to not take ownership of my own failures. That way of life was okay until my calling started to overshadow my negativity.

Every time someone asked me what I wanted to be when I grew up, my answer was a psychologist or psychiatrist because I wanted to help others and make the world a better place. Still today my answer is that I want to help others and make a difference in the world. My dream and inner thoughts were counterproductive to one another. I first had to believe in myself before I could help others.

During counseling and my own personal research—reading every self-help book that I could get my hands on—I started to realize how fortunate I had been. Yes, I had some traumatic events in my early childhood that were hard to carry, but I also had people who loved me and cared about my future. Those people spoke faith and encouragement into my life even when I wasn't ready to accept it.

When I was finally in a place where I could fully appreciate the positive people and experiences I've encountered, my mindset started to change. Being given up for adoption was hurtful, but it was also beautiful. Someone else chose to love me and care for me. They made a conscious decision to support me, nurture me, and stand with me for the rest of their lives. They didn't hide my adoption from me. They didn't keep my biological parents from seeing me. They put me first. That's what I consider unconditional love.

Looking at the complete picture of my childhood, I realized that it wasn't all bad. It wasn't all painful. It was also precious and loving. I'm eternally grateful that my birth parents gave me to my grandparents. That was the best gift they could have given me, a life surrounded by people who loved me and encouraged me.

I realized that our friends and neighbors invested in me too, not because it was convenient for them to have a young child following them around or showing up at their house but because they wanted to be positive influences in my life. They wanted to instill in me the faith that I could accomplish anything I set my mind to. They gave freely of their time in hopes that I would one day hear the words of encouragement they spoke into my life.

Those experiences and memories are what I now draw upon when I think of my childhood. I no longer allow the negative or hurtful times to overshadow the positive. The people who hurt me and my family, intentionally or not, do not deserve control over my life today. Instead, I use those instances as a learning opportunity for me to be better and do better than I was treated.

Growing up in Neon, I learned what it meant to care for others and provide when someone couldn't do for themselves. I understood what it meant to put in a hard day's work of manual labor and to still come home and complete a never-ending to-do list around the house. I watched as neighbors became family.

I witnessed what it meant to be a volunteer, to give of your time freely, and to care for others' well-being. I watched as my dad and brother served in the Neon Volunteer Fire Department as volunteers. They worked normal jobs, took care of their family, and still showed up for the community. I also witnessed firsthand how a community can show up for you.

During John's funeral and my dad's open-heart surgery, the community surrounded us, loved on us, and took care of us when we couldn't do it for ourselves. Family and friends carried food, gifts, and money to our home during two Christmases in a row. They didn't expect or want anything in return, only to help ease our pain. I remember how Mom and Dad smiled so graciously, and was truly humbled by our neighbors' support.

I knew then that was the type of person I wanted to be. I wanted to help others and give back no matter the cost. Because when I was a little girl, that support meant the world to me. To transform from that little girl to the woman I am now wasn't easy. It wasn't fast, and it wasn't foolproof. I made mistakes. I slid backward, and I gave up.

The reason I continued to get back up and try again was because of my "why." Above all else in the world, I wanted my children to have a childhood they didn't have to heal from. I wanted them to grow up self-assured, growth oriented, and compassionate—to always be kind and accepting of others, even when it wasn't easy. I wanted them to go further than me and to have an easier road to get there. For that to happen, I had to remove the roadblocks I put in front of our family. My mindset would either hinder their progression or catapult them forward. Knowing that I did not want to be the person holding them back, I decided it was time to change.

When it was time to heal and move forward, I remembered some of the people from my past—my family, neighbors, and friends—and the conversations, the walks around our hill, and the smiles every time I saw them. They were positive influences in my life that I drew on when I was ready to make a positive change. I thought of the people in my life currently who believed in me and valued my friendship. I knew they saw the me I wanted to be.

My second step forward focused on gratitude for the positive things in my life. When I started to look back at all the positive things that happened in my life, I was overwhelmed with the realization of how many moments I didn't fully cherish. I realized how my adopted family accepted me in my new role and loved me as if it was always meant to be that way. I recalled our neighbors who were always kind. I smiled at the memories I had with some of the volunteer fire department members and their families. Those memories and those people are who inspired me to be a better person. Their words of encouragement, belief, and friendship set the stage for me to be who I am today.

Religion helped me on my journey forward too. The first time I remember going to church was with our neighbor, Mary. It was extra work for her to take me with her to church, but she didn't mind. In fact, she offered to take me anytime. Our conversations were uplifting, and faith driven. Looking back, she wasn't planting a seed; she was planting a garden. Those seeds took time, but they did bloom.

I think of all the walks I tagged along with Alice, Lisa, and Carol, a mother, daughter, and daughter-in-law trio. I am sure they had more important things to discuss than a little kid's day, but they didn't act like it.

Instead, they listened to every story I rambled on about and answered every question that I asked. Each of them encouraged me in a different way. Alice always showed up when anything good or bad happened in my life. Graduations, weddings, deaths—for every major event in my childhood, she was standing nearby.

Carol was always soft spoken and kind. She had a way about her that immediately put you at ease, which is fitting—when I was looking for someone to read my rough draft, I thought of her. Not only had she watched me grow up and knew my family, but she was smart, well spoken, and most importantly, honest. I knew if anyone could help me move my book to the next level it was her. I sent her a message on Facebook, unsure of what her response would be, but I had high hopes that she would agree to read the jumbled-up words that I had poured out of myself.

When I received her response that she would be happy to read it, I was overjoyed and knew this book was now becoming a reality. She didn't email me feedback—she came to my house with a printed copy and talked with me face-to-face. She offered constructive suggestions and encouragement. Many of them were followed in this book.

Sweet Debra, who we met from the fire department, was much younger than Mom, but she turned out to be another friend throughout the years. Her gift of sewing provided me with an old-timey outfit for the Mountain Heritage Days for several years. Her support later followed us to the hospital where she worked. After Dad was diagnosed with colon cancer, he had regular colonoscopies, and Debra was right there with us. She would visit with us in the waiting room and often take me to the dining room to give Mom a break.

Judy and Mom's friendship may have formed while both volunteering with the Neon Fire Department, but it extended far past those days. When it was time for me to tour Clinch Valley College, now UVA Wise, Judy volunteered to take me and Mom. She helped us navigate the campus, asked questions that we didn't think of, and made us feel at ease. She was our calm in a pool of nerves.

The ties that wove us together in our small community know no distance. Our town was far more than just another coal community. In Neon neighbors were family, and generational roots were embedded as deep as an oak tree. Neon offered me safety and security during the hardest days of my life. The town I called home for the first 18 years of my life saved me when I needed it the most.

So, I share those stories to say I may not have had certain family members in my life, but I had others who willingly supported and encouraged me. I realized that my self-worth wasn't based off who wasn't in my life but who was.

Take some time and think of the people who have shown up in your life that didn't have to, the people who offered a word of encouragement, attended your sporting events, helped you with homework, or pushed you. Those people chose to be there for you. They saw you as worthy and competent. See yourself that way.

Being grateful replaced my bitterness. Once the bitterness started to be pushed aside, I felt more confident and participated less in comparison syndrome. I didn't say as often, "It must be nice," or "I will never be able to do what they do." I started saying, "Hmm, I wonder how I could accomplish that?" That's a powerful transition to recognize that you are capable of worthy accomplishments.

With my confidence improving, I finally allowed myself to acknowledge my dreams, not just daydream about them but acknowledge the possibility of achieving them. That acknowledgment led to a list of goals. There is a difference between dreams and goals. Goals are something you're working toward, whereas dreams are only in your imagination. I was ready to stop dreaming and start accomplishing.

CHAPTER 31
Finding Confidence

I was no longer too afraid to try for my goals or tell others what I hoped to accomplish.

My third step forward was to let go of the past and no longer allow the negativity or heartache to overshadow the love and good memories that I have. Forgiveness for myself and others didn't come easily. It took time and a lot of self-evaluation.

Through years of self-evaluation and headstrong confrontation with other loved ones, I am growing to understand I cannot control every aspect of my life. If you ask some of my loved ones, they may disagree with that statement, but I am trying. To prevent further tragedy or pain, I used to try to micromanage every small detail with contingencies in place for any possible variable. The urge is still there and as strong as ever; the only difference is my willingness to acknowledge it and attempt to rectify it.

I feel that my need for control came from losing John the way I did. Had I handled the situation differently, the outcome may have been different. I feel responsible for not realizing the dire situation and evaluating all possible outcomes before I walked away. No one in my family put the responsibility on my shoulders—I was never told that had I not left, John would still be alive. I placed that responsibility on myself.

That mindset has caused more arguments and hurt feelings than I can ever capture. Even when I can openly admit that I cannot control everything, I still try. So, I say that mindset is still a work in progress, one that

I will rectify so I can become more laid back—maybe when I am 90, but who's counting?

In all seriousness, I try to hold on to the fact that John would not have deceived us in such a grave way intentionally. Either he was so intoxicated that he didn't comprehend what he was saying, or he was so far gone mentally that he couldn't stay even for us. I can't imagine being in his shoes, looking at my heartbroken family, and still pulling the trigger; he must have felt desperate and defeated. For that, my heart breaks.

I am no longer mad at him, only heartbroken that he suffered as he did. No one should feel their only option is suicide. I still carry all of our pain with me but hopefully in a healthier way. I use the pain that each of us went through as a guide for how to treat others.

I know that he loved us and that the sober John wasn't selfish, but the drunk John was different—he was angry and spiteful and jealous. But I love him, because at one point he was my Big Daddy.

I accepted that holding on to past wrongs and heartache was only detrimental to me and my family. By staying angry, I was allowing their actions to control me years later, and that was not okay. Why should I allow anything to have so much control over my life? I had to forgive them to move on. I had to release the anger and animosity so that I could be happy. I did it for myself and my family.

Everyone's path to forgiveness will be a little different. I share mine only as an example of how I did it. I started intentionally listening for that little voice that crept in being a negative Nancy, and I squashed it before it had the chance to take center stage. I wrote down affirmations until my hand hurt from rewriting those same ones daily. I read self-help books and took notes like it was a college class. *Girl, Wash Your Face* and *Girl, Stop Apologizing* by Rachel Hollis and *The Morning Miracle* by Hal Elrod were the first books that resonated with me. They are the books that helped me find a way from self-deprivation to action.

Daily devotionals became an everyday ritual for me. No matter how busy my day was, I carved out a few minutes to read the daily message.

Two of my favorite daily devotionals are *All in All Journaling Devotional* by Sophie Hudson and *The One Year Daily Acts of Kindness Devotional* by Julie Fisk, Kendra Roehl, and Kristin Demery. The *All in All Journaling Devotional* features thought-provoking questions that were sometimes hard to answer. Identifying my shortcomings and weaknesses wasn't for the faint of heart, but to grow, I had to do it. Some of my answers were eye opening and laid the groundwork to enable me to see where I needed to change.

The One Year Daily Acts of Kindness Devotional was inspiring and motivating to make a difference in the world, even a small one. The simple act of doing something for someone else improved my mood as much as it did for the other person. I prayed for God to help me forgive myself and others. I asked for help and strength to overcome my past and to have grace for myself and others. I begged him to help me realize a future without heartache and one of joy.

I made a conscious effort to no longer compare myself to others. I finally accepted that each of us is designed to run our own race in our own time. Comparing myself to others would only hinder my progression. Every time that bitterness edged its way back into my thoughts, I paused and worked through the thought. I talked to myself as I would have my children: "You are two different people, with two different goals and paths; one cannot be compared to the other." When my mind drifted back to previous wrongs, I recited, "Those incidents do not define you. They define them." I didn't just say these words to say them; I meant them, and I believed them.

Slowly, past wrongs were released from my mind. That gradual release allowed me to forgive others and even find empathy and sympathy for some of them. It's powerful when you can change your point of view and realize that someone else was struggling when they hurt you. It doesn't dissolve what they did, but it makes it easier to forgive them.

With my why (the reason I wanted to change) center stage in my life, I transformed my dreams into obtainable goals. The first goal I set for myself was to research bachelor programs that I could enroll in and still work full-time. I looked at four different universities, where I compared the cost, the time commitment, and job-placement percentage to determine which one was the best fit for me. I didn't ask for others' opinions or suggestions—I trusted myself and my research. I ultimately decided on King College, now King University, because it was close to home and offered online classes; plus the cohort was only a year and a half.

My self-doubt started with the same song and dance that it had belted out throughout my life: Your grades aren't good enough, you're not smart enough, blah, blah, blah. This time I didn't listen to it. Putting a face to my self-doubt persona allowed for me to laugh at it more than take it seriously. I imagined the commercial where the germs are setting up residence in someone's lungs, then the medicine comes in and pushes them out. The look on their faces at that minute is what I envision my self-doubt persona having when I speak faith into myself.

My previous college transcripts were subpar, but my admissions letter left it all on the table. I was open and honest about my previous failures and the desire to change. I laid it all on the line, describing how much it would mean to me to graduate with a bachelor's degree. I concluded with my desire to make a difference in the world. Here's a quote from my personal statement:

As a single mother I understand the importance of self-respect, determination, and self-reliance. I feel a sense of responsibility to myself and to my son to demonstrate that someone can always improve. Being seen as a future leader in February 2010 I was nominated and accepted into the Forward Wise County Program, sponsored by the Wise County Chamber of Commerce. I graduated from the program in May 2010.

I did have the opportunity to attend college after high school but did not finish. I think about that decision often and regret it. I was young and impulsive. Now I am ready to finish what I started all those years ago. I am ready to be someone that I am proud of, but more importantly someone that my son will be proud of. My hope is that you will give me the opportunity to make a difference.

Ultimately, I was accepted into the program. That email may have been the most exciting thing that I have ever received in my inbox. I read it multiple times, and each time I felt that twinge of excitement in my heart.

Of course, self-doubt started to weasel its way back in again. It tried to play on my nervousness. Again, I didn't allow it to stay. I may have entertained it a little longer than I should have by thinking, I haven't studied in years. I'm a single mom and working full-time. I don't have enough time. While those thoughts were running through my brain, I realized it was mine to either achieve or fail. It was solely up to me and my grit if I would complete the program. I smiled because I knew I was ready for the challenge. I knew my whys for giving my son and myself a better life were more significant than my why not.

I did it when it was hard. I did it when I thought I couldn't. I cried. I slammed my books and wanted to give up. But then I went back and started over with fresh eyes. I didn't allow myself to give up. I didn't allow the negativity that was rushing through my mind to win. Your why must be stronger than your why not, and mine finally was. As I mentioned in an earlier chapter, college was difficult but oh so rewarding. Graduating with a college degree gave me the confidence that I needed. For me, it changed everything.

Your goal changer may not be going to college. Your goal changer may be something totally different. That's the great thing about our world; everyone is different, and everyone places value differently. Identify your goal changer and work toward it, even when it's hard and even when you're tired. Accomplishing it will change your mindset.

I was no longer too afraid to try for my goals or tell others what I hoped to accomplish. I didn't hide from opportunities—instead I put myself out there and tried. I didn't always succeed. I failed and made mistakes, but I kept trying. I had volunteered for the American Cancer Society for around eight years before I was finally hired as a Relay For Life community manager. Accepting that job was surreal to me. I was finally working for a company that was making a huge impact on cancer research and patient outreach. I was honoring my mom's memory and still fighting for her. At the time it was my dream job.

As the year went along, I realized that it was a dream job, just at the wrong time. The job required a lot of time away from my family, and that was something I wasn't prepared to do. My son needed to have me home more than I needed that job. So, after my one year, I turned in my notice with a full heart. I had made friends that would last a lifetime. I had learned more about celebrating the wins and fighting with a die-hard determination than I knew possible. I left that job with a new lease on life because of those I had surrounded myself with.

Life wasn't all smooth sailing for me after that. I still struggled with depression and self-doubt occasionally. The difference was I recognized it and didn't allow it to control my life. When I saw myself struggling, I went back to counseling again, because I knew it worked when I let my inhibitions down and was honest and open. The difference this time is I went close to home, because I was no longer embarrassed about asking for help. You shouldn't be either. It takes a strong person to recognize they need help to overcome something in their life.

My husband, Jamie, and I have been married for nine years. He and I complement each other perfectly. I am the big-picture person in our relationship, whereas he pays attention to details. Together we have built a life that we love and are proud of. We overcame the hard times together and celebrated every win. We have encouraged our kids to chase their dreams, even the big, crazy ones that seem impossible. Avery is nine years old and full of spunk. She played soccer and basketball, and she cheered and danced. With each new activity that she wanted to try, we've encouraged her to do her best. I know she's young and her interests may change, but for now, she is excelling in soccer and dance. We will do everything we can to further her skills without pushing her too hard.

Braden is now 16 years old and has been a part of Jamie's life since Braden was three. When Jamie was first introduced to Braden, he referred to Jamie as "Friend" for months. We all look back and laugh at how fast

Braden took up with Jamie. Jamie didn't have to take such an interest in Braden, but he did. From early on Jamie has loved Braden like a son and treats him as such, in both the good and bad.

In seventh grade Braden developed a love for politics that couldn't be dampened by anything else. He read every book and watched every YouTube video that was available to him. Truly he was a walking encyclopedia for politics. Jamie and I both worried about him taking on a career in such a volatile environment but knew that we had to support him.

Braden applied and was accepted as a Virginia House Page during his freshman year of high school. He was one of a select group chosen to live and work in Richmond during the 2022 house session. It was a dream come true for him. If he was scared or homesick, he hid it well. All I could see was excitement in him. It was a nightmare for me. I couldn't imagine leaving him in a big city five-plus hours away from me. What if he needed me? What if he got sick? The list of what ifs could have gone on for days.

I didn't allow my worries to stop him from chasing his dream. Instead, Jamie and I both supported him. On the day we left him in the hotel room, I knew he would be okay. We had given him the encouragement and knowledge to handle any obstacle that he faced. He was ready for the biggest adventure of his life. He excelled while there, serving as the mock speaker for the page house debate. I am so incredibly proud of him and know that he will accomplish big things in this world.

Our kids pay attention to us. If they see us going for our dreams, they will too. We showed Braden that it was possible, and we encouraged him to take the leap. I believe both of our kids will go further than us because of how we approach life and the obstacles we face.

While the world was shut down with COVID-19, I used that time to start writing this book. My first draft wasn't great. I had truly brain dumped all my thoughts into an 80,000-word document. It was a lot of rambling and very little cohesiveness. For it to be what you are reading now took a lot of work. To improve my craft, I started reading books about how to write a memoir—documentation about action words and sentence structure. I read every memoir that I could to serve as examples of structure and flow. Then I went back to what I had written and started piecing it together paragraph by paragraph.

I wasn't a very good reader or writer until I decided I was going to write this book. So, instead of giving up, I put in the hard work to figure it out. My first draft was a mess, and my second draft was still poorly written, but I kept editing. When I finally had it in a place that I was proud of, I hired an editor. His editorial review gave me the validation that I needed. My hard work had paid off.

In the process I found a passion that I didn't know I had. I absolutely love reading and writing. It's something that I believe I was called to do. If it's a dream of yours, don't quit. Take a break. Ask for help. But never quit. The gratification will be worth it.

In the middle of writing my book, Jamie and I decided to open a gym in our hometown. I was all in, ready for the challenge, while Jamie was the cautious one who I continually pushed. Make no mistake, he wanted to open the gym as well. It had been a dream of his. He was just more cautious than I was.

At this point, we've been open for a year and a half. Our success is far greater than we ever hoped for. That success is because of the amazing staff and members who call our gym a second home. You can feel the support and nonjudgment in the gym. It doesn't matter if you are just starting your fitness journey or have been training for years, there is a place for you there. At some point the gym morphed from ours to theirs. They are the reason the gym is successful. They are the reason that the gym continues to grow, and we love them for it. They are the reason we will do everything we can to maintain and improve the gym. They are the ones who give us the strength and drive to keep going.

Dreams may evolve over the years, as mine did, and that's okay. I may not be the psychologist or psychiatrist that I had dreamed of being when I was a kid, but I am still helping people. I am still making a difference in others' lives. That is what I truly wanted to do. I'm grateful for the road that brought me here. It gives me the ability to understand, encourage, and forgive others.

It's my hope this book will encourage you that anything is possible with hard work and tenacity—that you can be the person that you dream of being. Nothing but you is holding you back. You dictate your future.

Acknowledgments

First and foremost, thank you to my fantastic family. My husband, Jamie, has offered support and encouragement at every turn in my writing journey. My two children, Avery and Braden, have been understanding and encouraging during this process. Nothing means more than when your young daughter hugs you and tells you she is proud of you.

Thank you to my brother, who stepped in to be a second dad when he didn't have to be. I am grateful that he pushed me to be the best person I could be. Even though reliving the past wasn't easy for him, he still answered every question for me.

Thank you to my extended family for including me when I wasn't approachable. Thank you for loving me at a distance that I was comfortable with. I am grateful to each of you.

Thank you to all my neighbors and supporters while I was growing up. Your guidance, words of wisdom, and support may have taken time to resonate with me, but without them, I would not be where I am today. You are all so loved.

Thank you, Carolyn, for reading my very rough draft and investing enough time in my success that you drove over to meet with me in person. You went over every chapter and suggestion. Thank you for believing in me then.

Thank you to my childhood best friend, Tina. You were my saving grace from kindergarten to adulthood. Thank you for reading my memoir and giving me the feedback and support I needed.

Thank you, Jessica, for capturing the perfect cover photo. You have a gift of bringing a vision to life.

Thank you, Ashlyn, for the beautiful sketches of a mother and daughter holding hands.

Machelle, thank you will never be enough. You read and reread every chapter I wrote. You helped me with my website design, social media posts, and everything. Your friendship is more than I deserve. I am so grateful to you.

Laura, you are a true friend—always there, always loyal, always encouraging. You are a gift, and I am so grateful for you. Thank you for all the encouragement and advice. Thank you for picking up the pieces when I couldn't do it.

Jennifer and Joni, you both came into my life at the perfect time and are always encouraging and supportive. You truly helped in every way that you could. Thank you for all the help and advice.

Megan, thank you for reading my very rough draft and encouraging me every step of the way. Your encouragement and excitement for my memoir helped to move this book forward. Thank you for rereading the chapters as I edited them to improve my craft.

Stephanie and Jennifer thank you for reading my rough draft and providing the best feedback.

Thank you Jessica for being one of my biggest supporters throughout the years. Even though you are not a reader, thank you for taking the time to read my memoir and give me feedback.

Thank you Amy for all of your support and encouragement throughout our friendship and this process.

Call to Action

Visit my website: www.brandicoxauthor.com.

Let's be friends on Facebook: https://www.facebook.com/brandicoxauthor.

Follow me on Instagram: https://www.instagram.com/brandicoxauthor.

Check out my growing list of favorite inspirational memoirs and self-help books: https://www.brandicoxauthor.com/additionalreading.

Find additional mental health resources at https://www.brandicoxauthor.com/resources.

Printed in the USA
CPSIA information can be obtained
at www.ICGtesting.com
CBHW020739201223
2789CB00002B/3

9 798988 792505